Essays on Furries by the Most Prominent

Members of the Fandom

Edited by Thurston Howl

A THURSTON HOWL PUBLICATIONS BOOK

ISBN 978-0990890263

FURRIES AMONG US: ESSAYS ON FURRIES BY THE MOST PROMINENT MEMBERS OF THE FANDOM

Copyright © 2015 by Thurston Howl

First Edition, 2015. All rights reserved.

A Thurston Howl Publications Book
Published by Thurston Howl Publications
thurstonhowlpublications.com
Nashville, TN

jonathan.thurstonhowlpub@gmail.com

Cover design by Thurston Howl
Cover art by Rukis © 2015
Title page art by Nyareon © 2015
Profile illustrations by Sabretoothed Ermine © 2015

Printed in the United States of America
10 9 8 7 6 5 4 3 2 1

Vivat animali. In nostro cordibus vivat animali.
Ubi colliderent duos mundos tenue est.

ACKNOWLEDGEMENTS

"'By the Numbers': Comparing Furries and Related Fandoms" by Courtney Plante. © 2015.

"First Furry Convention at Califur 2008, A Memoir" by Covrin Dallas. © 2015.

"Furcons: the Ins and Outs" by Zantal Scalie. © 2015.

"Furry Erotica" by Kyell Gold. © 2015.

"Fursuiting and the Fandom" by Keefur. © 2015.

"Introduction" by Thurston Howl. © 2015.

"Marginalization of Anthropomorphic Identities: Public Perception, Realities, and 'Tails' of Being a Furry Researcher" by Sharon E. Roberts. © 2015.

"My Experience with Furry Online Dating" by Takaa. © 2015.

"Social Furs: an Inside Look at How the Furry Fandom Socializes" by Shoji. © 2015.

"Social Identity Perspective of the Furry Fandom" by Stephen Rysen. © 2015.

"The Furry Fandom as a Folk Group" by C. L. Methvin. © 2015.

"The Furry Fandom" by Nyareon. © 2015.

"The Fuzzy Notes of Furry Fingers" by Roo. © 2015.

"The History of Furry Publishing" by Fred Patten. © 2015.

"The Origins of the International Anthropomorphic Research Project" by Kathleen C. Gerbasi. © 2015.

"What Does Art Mean to the Furry Fandom?" by Zambuka. © 2015.

"Yiff? Murr?: Sex in the Furry Fandom" by Thurston Howl. © 2015.

CONTENTS

INTRODUCTION

Hello there. The name's Howl. I am an avid writer, a daily consumer of vanilla lattes, somewhere between the stereotypical twink and otter, and also a furry. What is a furry, you say? A sexual deviant? A man with extra hair on his chest? A nerd in a mascot suit? Well, why can't I very well be all three? Just kidding there. I am a folf dog, a fox-wolf-dog hybrid, that is. I have black fur with red on the top of my head, going down my back (it can all take quite a bit of patience to brush, I assure you). Look for the writer with the skinny jeans, the XS t-shirt, and either a red dog collar or a purple scarf (depends on the season really), and that's me.

In 2014, I contemplated my involvement in what has been collectively known as "the furry fandom" and realized that, for some odd reason, there has been little to no research into furries, what they are, how they operate, and how they compare to the common, modern myths about them. What a conundrum! So, I immediately began asking some of my friends in the fandom on their thoughts about having a book that contained writings from different furry experts and celebrities detailing what it actually means to be a furry. Most of them loved the idea, though I did receive some criticism that writing about it would alienate the fandom.

To counter this notion, I want to point out that this book serves two, and only two, purposes. On one paw, this book was written for furries, an exploration into different aspects of the fandom that some furries may have been curious about without knowing how to investigate. Even as a folf dog myself, I learned new things from many of the following articles! I even teared up at some of the anecdotes herein. On the other paw, this book can serve as a primer for non-furries if they are curious about what furries are. To those who worry that this book may lead to misinterpretations about what a furry is, note that even as I sit here typing this, glasses at the edge of my snout, I am not pretending to be an authority figure. This book contains many voices, including best-selling novelist Kyell Gold, the renowned artist Zambuka, the International Anthropomorphic Research Project, some fursuiters, some con-goers, and yes, I myself may have written one article for this little collection. What else is a folf to do on rainy days? Ultimately, whether you are a furry or a furry-to-be, please keep in mind that what being a furry means really is different for each individual.

Returning to the creation process, after finding enough contributors, I worked with each person on drafting, revising, proofreading, and copyediting their articles for your viewing pleasure. I have enjoyed working with each of them, and I hope you enjoy reading their words as well. Thurston Howl Publications spent about six months working with this team of contributors, and they all did this pro bone-o!

At any rate, now that you understand a little of the purpose and conception of this work, let me explain to you a bit about the organization following. The work shall start out to loosely define furry with Nyareon's article "The Furry Fandom." From there, the tiger Shoji shall start the discussion of the importance of the social life for furries, with Hypetaph's follow-up by arguing that furry is more than a fandom: it's also a folk group. After this introduction into furry social life, Kyell Gold and Fred Patten shall discuss furry literature, the publishing history, and even the specific genre of furry erotica. This is where I come in with a discussion of the common stereotype of "furries and sex," with Takaa explaining the furry dating scene. Afterward comes articles on specific aspects of the furry fandom, all important in their own way, including art, music, fursuiting, and furry conventions. The final articles are provided by the International Anthropomorphic Research Project on the psychological and sociological implications of the furry fandom. This collection will close with a brief bio on our two amazing artists, Rukis and Sabretoothed Ermine. Many of the following works are playful, informal, and, at times, sarcastic and ranty. Others are professional, academic, and quite well-informed. Because of the variance in styles throughout this book, some will naturally appeal to you more than others. I only hope that you will have gained something from them.

Hopefully, by the end of this book, you will have a much greater sense of the furry fandom. Maybe, I'll even see you around with your own pair of ears, collar, or tail, walking down the street or on the Web. On that note, if after reading this collection, you have questions you'd like to ask the contributors or myself, please feel free to contact my human-sona (the furless bugger) at jonathan.thurstonhowlpub@gmail.com. He is open to comments, suggestions, questions, and compliments on his scarf. Now, let's cross the boundary between humans and animals into a world of anthropomorphic beings, into the realm of furries. One paw at a time, ever onward.

Thurston Howl
Founder of Thurston Howl Publications

THE FURRY FANDOM
Nyareon

Nyareon is a small, feral purple Snow Leopard/Fox Hybrid (Snox Feopard for short) created and belonging to Charlie Kenward. Inspired by the Pokémon franchise, Nyareon is a tiny, cute, unique Eeveelution (term for the various evolutions of the Pokémon Eevee).

Her personality is always happy, upbeat and optimistic. You can often find her out in nature, hiding in the tall grass and playing with the little critters within. She is always smiling and welcoming and although she tries to avoid drama, it always seems to find her.

Her involvement in the fandom includes Art, Fursuiting, hosting her local Furmeets, running the What Is A Furry? *Facebook page and actively raising money for charity and inspiring a good public image of the Fandom.*

The Furry fandom is a puzzling experience to people on the outside of this diverse and unique fandom, but what is it all about? The term "Furry" directly relates to anthropomorphic animals; this means animals with human features or characteristics such as human speech and body language but with an animal appearance.

Furries have been in the media for over half a century; in fact many notable furries originally came to being thanks to the imagination of the animator Walt Disney who created the most iconic Furry characters such as Mickey Mouse and Goofy. Even after Walt's death, the Disney company continued to create unique anthropomorphic characters to capture and inspire the minds of many, blending the wild and wonderful animal world with the familiar and relatable human world.

There are two types of Furry character: one is anthropomorphic, the other is feral. As the name suggests, feral furries are based on more realistic animal skeletal structures, such as walking on all fours or having more true-to-life facial detail rather than the cartoony counterparts commonly seen with anthropomorphic bodies. Examples of some famous anthropomorphic furries include Sonic the Hedgehog, Bugs Bunny, Tom and Jerry, and Tigger. Feral Furry examples include Balto, Scooby Doo, Bolt, Simba, and Bambi. Pokémon also played a large part in the creation of many fursonas.

The introduction of furries into the media caused many people to see into the animal world through the eyes of these characters; as children we are influential and have strong imaginations: we enjoy exploring and playing in nature. These characters who are human in mind but animal in body can strike a chord with many of us who like to imagine a world where animals are as advanced as humans yet maintain their features which are fantasy-like to us, such as tails, wings, and ears.

The word "Furry" not only relates to the characters themselves, but also to people who are fans of said characters. Any person who describes themselves as a Furry is referring to the title which is given to a fan of anthropomorphic characters:

this is where the Furry fandom gets its name. As a whole, the fandom started back in the 1980s with the majority of its popularity and exposure growing in the 1990s with artwork and media coverage. Many Furries joined the fandom thanks to the artistic aspect in which you can use inspiration from existing characters and begin creating your own, with so many animals, hybrids and fantasy creatures to explore personality possibilities: the ideas are seemingly endless.

The name given to a personal Furry character creation is "fursona" which is coined from Furry and persona. A fursona is an individual Furry's character, made from one or more animals that fan is interested in either for their specific personality traits or their appearance; often, a fursona is given markings or color schemes that resonate with the fan to create a unique looking character that is unique to that one person; this causes a fursona to become more personal on creation. In some ways, you could say a fursona is literally a cartoon Furry version of themselves they have made out of an accumulation of animals, colors, and patterns they feel matches their own personalities. The most common animals seen in the fandom are Felines, Canines, and Vulpines, but the inclusion of mythical and fantasy animals such as Gryphons, Dragons and Sergals has become increasingly popular in the fandom, and even some less common creatures such as Skunks, Newts and Pangolins. A lot of furries will enjoy creating a hybrid instead, combining mythical with existing and so on; there are endless possibilities, and there have been numerous unique and interesting creations which have taken the fandom by storm with people becoming fascinated by certain hybrids or brand new creations and partaking in their own version of these newly created species: examples are Angel Dragons and Sparkledogs.

The fursuiter who made the Angel Dragons popular is known worldwide throughout the fandom and goes by the fursona name of Telephone; not only is she hailed for being one of the most influential and talented fursuit actors, but she can also build adorable fursuits as well as partake in fursuit dancing competitions. Telephone's use of a custom-made fursuit squeaker has also helped expand the range in which people can act out their character and communicate without breaking the illusion of the character by speaking normally from inside the suit. Since her debut, she has been inspiring many furries and fursuit artists to improve their fursuit acting and communication skills.

Some furries see their fursona as an alter-ego, expressing themselves in ways they can't in normal society due to bullying and being judged, after being put down for being hyper, or too serious, or just plain different; many furries feel they were alienated from their peers, and thus some fursonas are simply representing that person's inner longing to be able to express and act how they want to, without being called out for it or picked on, because the fursona is what people see and is designed to match the traits. It doesn't draw the negativity like a human being in today's society. Feeling safe behind a fursona gives people that freedom because of its anonymous possibilities; you can finally express yourself without having people judging you on a personal scale.

Artwork has played a massive role in the creation of the fandom: it serves as most people's first port of call into the Furry world. There are Furry artists who only draw Furry specific pictures, usually of their own fursona or of a character they have created. Many furries take to the artistic side so as to develop and share their vision of their creations; those who are less talented will often pay to commission a more talented artist than them to draw their characters based on either a description or a reference sheet. Some artists have allowed free lineart to be accessible online so that people without the talent of drawing could use it as a template to begin a creation, adding their own colors and patterns and so can then present it as their reference sheet for future artwork.

Drawing artwork has enabled many people to develop and improve due to the desire to be as good as artists they aspire to match, following tutorials for all types of techniques, from basic sketching all the way through to complex shading effects and backgrounds. It also opens up a new window for business opportunities to the artists with the most influence and skill, with many people paying in the hundreds for reference sheets or very professional looking artwork and prints.

A large number of furries will attend events where they can meet and befriend other furries, wearing attire suited to the fandom in the form of attachable tails, ears, paws, or even an entire fursuit. These events are known as furmeets, with the larger, more annual ones being called Furry conventions. Furmeets typically happen as often as one day every month; some can be several months apart. The common activities at furmeets tend to involve mingling amongst each other, with artists taking to a small section of the venue to draw and sell artwork. Those in fursuits will likely be out greeting the public by the venue and having pictures taken. A few furmeets will include a "fursuit walk" in which those with fursuits, or those who fancy coming along, go for a scheduled hour long walk around the area; it is usually very well received by the public who pick up the carefree "why not?" attitude that the furwalks present. Furry conventions happen on a larger scale lasting for an extended weekend, with indoor fursuit parades, activities, dancing competitions, and usually the popular night time Furry rave party where furries can dress up in their fursuits or accessories and enjoy a rave with their friends. These conventions take place in hotels for the most part, and a lot of the visitors to these conventions tend to stay on-site in the hotel rooms provided.

Fursuits are the physical representation of a fursona or character, typically made from upholstery foam and faux fur. Many of the furries see these as the best form of realizing a fursona, and thus many want to have a fursuit. However due to the complexity in making a fursuit which is presentable and durable, many people end up looking to experienced and talented fursuit makers to create their fursuits. A standard fursuit will set most furries back roughly $1,000 dollars with the price steeply climbing, depending on its complexity in the pattern or accessories. Many fursuit makers stick to one type of fursuit; these types range and vary but the most common types are Toony, Realistic, and Quadsuit. Toony suits commonly feature large cartoon eyes, bold colours or patterns, and often don't feature leg padding so as to use the wearer's natural leg shape under the fur. Realistic suits often use fur that has been airbrushed to resemble far more realistic animal fur, patterns and spots, small animal-like eyes that the wearer sees through the tear ducts, and padded legs to give the impression of backward bending hind-legs (known as digitigrade). Quadsuits are specially made for the purpose of wearing and walking on all fours; they are usually realistic looking, with tube-like structures on the arms to level out the spine and make it a little easier to walk in. Currently the most expensive fursuit known is Cryo the Cyberwolf, costing a whopping $14,000 dollars (yes, you read correctly).

Many furries feel they can't afford a full fursuit; therefore the popular solution exists in partial suits. Partial suits (partials for short) feature a head, tail, foot paws, and hand paws with arm sleeves. They can be worn with normal clothing and saves on cost as arguably the most expensive part (being the body suit) is left out, saving the hassle of making a duct tape dummy in order to get the suit made to fit. Getting a partial also saves on a large portion of the costs and time consumption. Partials tend to go for around $500 dollars depending on complexity and work included. A lot of celebrities who are furries will attend conventions in fursuits to preserve their anonymity: you never know if the next fursuit you bump into could have a movie star hiding inside.

Something the fandom prides itself in is raising money for charity. The largest convention in the world at current is Anthrocon; in 2014 the convention helped raise over $32,000 for charity thanks to donations and fundraising from fursuiters and local businesses. Fundraising events are a perfect chance for furries to wear their suits in public without causing alarm, as well as helping and encouraging people to donate to the charities they are supporting thanks to the suit drawing attention to the event. Due to the alarming heat inside a fursuit, many fursuiters don't partake in strenuous activity when wearing their suits, so as to not overheat or damage the suit, the few exceptions to this are when fursuiters attend fur raves at conventions or dance competitions. Many fursuiters choose to install a fursuit cooling fan in the head of the fursuit to keep the airflow and help prolong their time in a fursuit, especially when actively moving a lot.

Due to the massive diversity in the fandom, there are many types of furries who identify into different spectrums, some examples are Otherkin, Scalies, and Bronies. Scalies are furries without fur, i.e. lizards like to be identified as scaleys rather than furries. Bronies are adult fans of My Little Pony (some of the female fans prefer being called Pegasisters). They create characters based on the show and in many ways are seen as being part of the Furry fandom; however, some bronies do not wish to be associated under the title Furry. Otherkin feel a more spiritual connection into their choice of fursona, often believing that they are part-animal, either in mind or spirit, or partially human, or entirely non-human, akin to that of reincarnation. The majority of Otherkin relate to mythical creatures like angels, demons, or elvenkind.

The Furry fandom is constantly growing: its members thrive in its diversity, and this expanding nature is actively encouraging new members to join and experience a multitude of ways to express themselves however they feel most comfortable. There are many sides to the Furry Fandom. Be it art, costume making, acting, dancing, writing, or singing, there is always something new to experience and try out right around the corner.

SOCIAL FURS:
AN INSIDE LOOK AT HOW THE FURRY FANDOM
SOCIALIZES
Shoji

Shoji is currently a biology student at Kalamazoo College. He has published a furry short story for a recent charity anthology: "The Forest, the River, and the Warmth of the Pack" (Wolf Warriors, 2014). He has also been in the fandom for over five years and has been to several furry meetups and two furry conventions. He has been an active participant in the Los Angeles furry community. Recently, Shoji has taken on an editing position at Thurston Howl Publications.

Even in the socially awkward realm of the nerd fandom, you do need to interact with others to really make it a fandom in the first place. From the greymuzzles to the tabletop gamers to the boozy furs, the furry fandom has huge variety to choose from. A myriad of locations and forms of interaction add even more to the varieties of connections between furries and in this article I'll take a look at the ways furries communicate and the ways interactions between people and groups have shaped the fandom and continue to shape it today. To begin, I'd like to make a primary distinction between the two furry fandoms: one of them exists in meetings with other furries in person at cons or furmeets, and the other exists in the online realm. These are obviously not mutually exclusive spheres of the furry fandom and at least in this day and age, it would be very difficult to have one without the other. Each side of the fandom has its own drawbacks and benefits, but any furry who has experienced both of them can likely say they're thankful for having both options.

The majority of us usually start things out online; we run into some of Uncle Kage or Two's videos on YouTube; we run across some Thundercats fan art, or maybe some of us see anthro spinoffs of My Little Pony. Regardless of how, the typical proto-furry gets curious while browsing online and suddenly they get slapped across the face with the fluffy paw that is the furry fandom. So now whoever's looking in is scrolling through the tons and tons of images and stories in the backlogs of FA, InkBunny and Sofurry. They react in several ways. Some go off to Roleplay forums where they learn how to paw off or they hang with the artists and figure out that you can make a bit of change on the side drawing; some run into the writers; some of them get into group moderation. Whatever a fur-in-training does, the assimilation is usually complete when they find a fursona for themselves.

The fursona: the great unifying theme of the furry fandom, and the lens through which much of anyone's socializing as a furry will take place. Fursonas vary from person to person and they usually fall under being a species that fits with a person's tastes and personality and they often represent an idealized version of who they want to be. If anyone takes a casual image search on any furry site (but please don't go to the front page of FA), they will hardly find any trace of frailty or advanced age or overweightedness in any of the furry characters. Most fursonas are young, athletic or slim, and physically nicer looking, the ladies often show more curves and cleavage, and the guys have pretty nice equipment between the legs. The fursona then becomes an expressive, good-looking and personalized entity through which a furry presents themselves as they want to be seen.

The high level of personality among furries and the fursonas through which they express themselves is a driving force for a refreshing level of kindness and acceptance among members of the fandom. Being part of the furry fandom offers a haven for many young nerds and artists. Members of minorities and people who had been outcast can often turn to the fandom for support, and I can speak from personal experience that being a furry helped me come to terms with all the pressures and difficulties of being a young gay male, and I even fell in love with a very special husky along the way. I applaud and thank the furry fandom every day for its level of support and tolerance to everyone. No one gives you a hard time for being gay, straight, transgender, lesbian, bisexual. I've made friends with furs from all walks of life, all ages and all kinds of personalities, and I'll always dearly love the openness of the fandom.

I discovered a great deal of this openness initially through the vast online furry roleplaying community. Forums like SoFurry chat, Chatzy, F-list and others provide furries with a limitless place to express their fantasies and imaginations. The level of creativity here is massive to say the least, and without a doubt I can attribute my own abilities with writing to having been involved in online roleplay. Furries socialize through roleplay openly and often meet many of their close friends and even romantic partners through the process. Roleplay sites enable many forms of sexual expression, and many areas of interest that are commonly seen as slightly taboo in mainstream society are both accepted and welcome because everyone in the chat has their own brand of weird, and it really isn't worth anyone's time to judge when they're just as odd as the next guy.

Online roleplay, particularly in the sexual realm, lets furries embody their desires into their fursona and liberate themselves from the norms of everyday life. In a roleplay, no one cares if you're overweight, a certain race, have more or less money or even what age you are to most degrees. Everyone's online to just have fun and express themselves and this often lets the furs involved act openly and with a great deal of tolerance and kindness when in an online circle. By acting as their fursona, the strong, attractive, sexy, popular person they either see themselves as or they wish that they were. Playing as a muscular leopard or a cute playful fox can be awfully therapeutic to the often sheltered nerds that make up the fandom as it lets them see that their fantasies are perfectly okay, and I've seen many instances of furries in chat rooms acting as therapists because the online fandom can also become a safe place where furries who are falling into hard times in their real life can reach out for help and support from their friends online. Talking to friends in the fandom online helped me to come out as gay, and gave me a bit of extra drive when I was feeling upset about various issues on a particular day, and I also have helped many friends when they were in the midst of some very troubling times.

Regardless of the way anyone reading this has found their way into the fandom, the basic principle and greatest advantage of the online fandom is pretty clear: anyone can get into it and has access to it. You can be in the middle of Banjotown, America and looking at *Lion King* fanfics when you're done milking the cows, or you can be across the ocean from someone in Brisbane and talk to them about your common interests with Nerf guns. The online furry community will always be the larger of the two sides of the fandom, and in that plane, physical distance doesn't matter because you can share your ideas and talk to other furries from anywhere.

The situation at hand when people from far-flung areas socialize virtually but possibly do not know how to socialize with others in person can be one of the more unpleasant side effects of the online nature of the majority of the fandom. Many furries indeed are more akin to shy basement-dwelling nerds than to muscled dragons or wolves or miscellaneous mammals that they present themselves online as. The phenomenon of the socially awkward furry is one that is well-known to many of us, and I can admit that I was probably one hell of an awkward tiger when I stepped into my first furmeet. Once a furry makes their way past the online realm, they often make their way to their first local furmeet. The typical furmeet usually takes place in an open public area like a park, and occasionally a generous furry will invite the local fandom to get together and have a party at their house. The things that people are dressed in usually vary greatly. Most attendees to a furmeet wear badges with a portrait of their fursona with their furry name as a way to associate themselves in person with their fursona and online presence. Furries will often refer to themselves and others by their furry alias and species.

Furries tend to separate into different sub-groups when at a furmeet. There's often a group that is into movies and will congregate by a TV or video player to watch movies like *The Lion King* or *The Secret of Nimh* or *Robin Hood* (especially *Robin Hood* because it has a bound fox in it). Oftentimes, the sci fi nerds and the furries in attendance who are fans of *My Little Pony* will be in their own groups, watching the shows they enjoy most. In other areas, there's a group of furries who are the more artistic ones, and they often sit with sketch pads and draw and often collaborate on and critique each other's art. There's usually an area somewhere that has a space for dancing and music, and there's also typically places where attendees play tabletop games and video games on consoles. Some popular card games include Cards Against Humanity, Magic: The Gathering and more furry games, like Nord Guard and Furoticon. These game choices often act as an extension to the social roleplaying community online into interactions at a furmeet.

For those members of the fandom who don't have practical means of getting to a furmeet, recent developments in online social networking have worked very positively in their favor. The ability to chat via live webcam on Skype has allowed furries from far flung areas to get together and interact face to face and speaking personally, it's one of the single greatest tools both inside and out of the fandom. Talking to someone face to face allows both involved to get a better sense for each other and how they would behave in a real interaction. Skype is particularly helpful for long-distance friendships and relationships (as I am well aware) because it's more honest to social interaction than the easy fakability of voice chats and the even further distance of talking through text. For furries that live far from their friends or romantic interests, Skype calls and other means of video interaction allow for more open socialization and connection with others in an almost completely in person basis. This helps many furs stay connected to the outside world and makes a nice time hanging out with friends, the push of a button away. I have made some very close friends both local and long distance over Skype calls, and group chats and video calls are what keep countless relationships alive across long distances.

In my five years of experience in the furry fandom, I've gone through multiple phases of the social furry experience. I started off just talking to people in different chat groups and began making friends online, then moved my way through roleplay forums where I met some of my closest friends in the fandom and got scooped into a relationship across three time zones. After all this took place, I found a group of local furries from Los Angeles and started to attend furmeets and have all kinds of fun times with the friends I made locally. If there's one thing I've learned from talking to people across different regions and different areas of the fandom, it's that the many ways furries get together and talk to each other is what shapes this dynamic and colorful fandom.

THE FURRY FANDOM AS A FOLK GROUP
Hypetaph

Who is this freak?

Is... is he a wolf? And is that... a battery?

Hypetaph – called either Hype or 'Taph – is a gray wolf furry, fitted with an external battery modification along the upper spine. Wires course from this protrusion into the neck, collar bones, hips, and base of his tail. One can imagine how difficult it can be for him to wear shirts.

Art, literature, and writing are all of interest to Hype, and as such the furry fandom is an inarguably inviting community; he has yet to leave, after all. Sometimes he glitches, as electrical things often do, but th

th-aaa

thhhhhhh

that is nothing one can avoid. 'Taph makes his way through malfunctions, puts his pants on one leg at a time, often skips the top, and continues wagging his wired tail.

Not completely unheard of, the subculture dubbed the "Furry Fandom" has become somewhat prevalent in modern media, earning spots as the plot points in television and movies, focuses in pieces of art, as well as just generally becoming more widely-known, where once the immediate response may have simply been "what?" Given that I am a member of the fandom, have recently had first-person experience at a nearby convention, and am able to and have spoken to numerous others involved through various social media hubs, the research presented will not only explain the subculture in its raw form but also elaborate on its interpretation by others to illustrate the difference between what it is, what it is perceived to be, and enforce its standing as a developing folk group. Despite the fandom's recent establishment, it maintains unique dialectic variations, places value on particular topics exclusive to its own inner workings, and is met with confusion by outside groups, arguably one of the most defining factors of a folk group, whether old or in development.

Considered deviant by the more vocal internet masses, this particular folk group maintains a very familial community, in which many people can conglomerate regardless of differences under the same, shared interest in anthropomorphic animals, art, and self-embodiment. Recently, television shows such as *CSI* and *Taboo* (which paints a fairly evident opinion of the subculture in the production title alone) have utilized the fandom as a means to further negative stereotypes while simultaneously providing false information (undoubtedly for increased viewership). Not one minute into the program, *Taboo* claims furries "are people who believe they are part human, part animal" (National Geographic Channel 2012) despite that being a separate community called Therians (which will be briefly defined later). *CSI* delves deeper into incorrectness in an episode entitled "Fur and Loathing" that portrays the entirety of the fandom as an explicitly sexual fetish. While I will not deny a sexual aspect, to categorize the entire subculture as centered on such practice is a colossal exaggeration; every subculture has some aspect of fetishism, though that does not make the primary focus of said folk group specifically sexual.

What it means to be part of this subculture cannot be decisively defined, as there belongs to the members large amounts of individual jurisdiction for what it means *to them*, though a common factor among all definitions is identifying (whether online or in person) with a secondary (sometimes, even more than one extra) anthropomorphic persona—often called a "fursona," which resembles most accurately one's personal characteristics. I visited the social media hub Twitter and asked for the opinions of many other members of the subculture what it means to be part of the community. To no surprise, I received a wide variety of answers. Some were short and simple, describing it "like a second home… like a family as well. Where all my friends are" (Miko 2015), or "a place that allows me to be myself. To forget about my daily job and responsibilities, if only for a bit" (Zarroc 2015). Other answers were much lengthier, though just as valid:

> I define furries as a group or movement of people who like anthropomorphic animals and creatures, and they [demonstrate] their… passion for that in [different] ways, like painting, dancing, making music, histories, etc… [The] [f]andom, for me, is the action[s] that make furries… settle in that group. Making their fursonas, fursuits, badges, or things that… identify you. (Raya 2015)

The provided examples are few of many that were given, but all with personal inclusions and exclusions all centered on interaction or art with an anthropomorphic focus. To identify as a part of this community is to become part of a very specific—as stated above—family, though *the becoming* itself is very much a personal endeavor: there are no accepted guidelines to be had. It is through a surprisingly specific, outwardly bizarre, though common collection of interests in the anthropomorphic that binds otherwise unfamiliar individuals together—whether that is through escapism, combined differences, costuming, or a generally familial attitude toward one another; if you "ask twelve different furries what 'Furry' means to them... you're likely to get a dozen definitions" (Simo [2009?]), and I most certainly did.

I will not pretend to be an avid attender of conventions; however I did have the pleasure to visit the 2015 "Furry Weekend Atlanta" in Georgia and amongst the interviews with other convention attendees were numerous references to being part of one larger family or friendship. One of those I interviewed very confidently defined the fandom as "definitely a friendship thing, having a bunch of fun, rompin' around in animal suits" (Ebony 2015), and generally treating it as a playful part of oneself. Ebony was particularly thrilled at the responses given to the fursuits (as it sounds: full-body suits of anthropomorphic characters), reiterating that "nobody's doing any harm, the kids love it too, y'know—when people come up and they see *that* [at this point Ebony points to a detached fursuit head], they love it! ...it's just a really fun thing that people get to do and be themselves." As a researcher of the subculture, Stephen Reysen so accurately states members of the fandom are "largely motivated to be part of the community because the fandom affords furries a sense of belonging" that is largely unseen in other aspects of the individual's life. From artistic interests, to sexual and gender identification, the community is a massively inclusive familial structure—one convention-goer, dubbed "The Neon Fox," described it shortly and sweetly as having "a lot of big gay here, and it's very yiff-tastic, and I probably couldn't live without it."

Having read that last sentence, it would be more surprising than not if a reader not already affiliated with furries were already familiar with the term. "Yiff" is only one among many terms unique to the furry subculture, which has not only developed a small lexical extension, but also utilizes pre-existing words (typically associated with animals—and more specifically, animal *motions*) as an intricate means to further conversation. Words like "yip" and "bark" (among other onomatopoeic expressions) are used to represent happiness or excitement in most cases, while terms like "perks ears" or "wags tail" could identify curiosity. Similarly, one can "curls up" if tired, "droops tail" if sad, and numerous other colloquialisms that permeate the online vernacular of the furry fandom. While one may reasonably refrain from expressing these notions to one outside the subculture, to any comfortable members this is a regular practice, and sometimes the majority of a conversation will be conducted in this fashion as a playful banter to express emotion as opposed to collected thoughts. In the below figure, a short conversation between me and another fandom member shows how easily those familiar with the fashion can interact, substituting notions and implications in place of explicit purpose.

FIGURE 1. Image courtesy of R. Chimera.

In addition to onomatopoeic sounds and motion-implicit phrases exist other "folk speech" deviations from standard dialogue formats (Brunvand 1998, 73); the fandom has also developed a significant amount of unique, individual terms that bear no meaning outside the community. The phrase "greymuzzle" identifies one as an older member of the furry community, as if the fur around one's face is beginning to gray. The jab "fursecution" is a playful term for the ignorance of those outside the fandom that may express negative opinions of it—rarely if ever is this term used in any serious fashion (Simo 2015). Revisiting the term "yiff," it is a catchall term for nearly anything pornographic in nature within the fandom (Simo 2015). To have sex is to "yiff;" to watch porn is to "yiff;" erotic anthropomorphic writing is called "yiff;" more or less, the term is used as a means to identify pre-existing practices, but as a specifically furry-inclusive version: anyone can have sex, but only furries can yiff. "Therians"[1] as mentioned before, are a branching community that share some similarities with furries, but are wholly of a more spiritual inclination—where furries identify secondly with a particular animal, Therians are connected with said animal on a spiritual level: Therians can be furries, though not all furries are Therians. There are significantly more words in the lexicon of this folk group (far more than can be adequately encompassed in this research), though all of them are unique in the manner in which they often *only* apply to the fandom, with little to no room for this outside ownership.

A subdivision of language is the nature of jokes and the isolated fashion in which humor applies only to the group involved. A common jest among friends is playfully, purposely making a noise or reference inconsistent with one's fursona, as to imply a jab at that particular species. For example, were someone—let us say someone identifying as a tiger—to perhaps clumsily trip, after a laugh he might tack on "woof" to jokingly signify the excitable personality of dogs. More specifically, were someone eating and another person longingly eyeing the meal, one may tease "since when did you become a

---

[1] Separate from Otherkin, which is inclusive of mythological beings, such as dragons, chimeras, and the like. Therians are limited to existing animals.

raccoon?" as to indicate their scavenging habits. While jokes about animals are by no means a furry-exclusive concept, in the furry context they not only make humor of the referenced creature, but also at the identification of the quip's subject. The essence of banter is quintessential in depicting the values of a community: what can and cannot be made antics of and their significance to the present context.

Many jokes have deeper roots than the simple surface-level attributes of the particular animal. Foxes are very notorious within the subculture, as in the fandom's earlier days of conception ("earlier" being generally subjective, but in this context referring to the early 1990s) foxes were very prevalent in pornographic depictions. This lasted for a rather long time until the numbers and species inevitably grew alongside the community's popularity, though the stigma still remains. While foxes *are* traditionally considered cunning or seductive creatures (present in many Native American and East Asian folktales), the fox's status as an erotic symbol within the furry folk group is of an individualized origin. Thus, if one is to refer to another as a fox (who was not definitively a fox already) the implications of their sexual nature are apparent, though without negative stigma. Essentially, the idiom is a playful, acceptable way to openly talk about sexuality—a humorous derivative of the fandom's erotica.

Traditional folklorist Brunvand (1998) argues that great problems arise when folk groups are influenced by clothing industries (575), but with furries this merely sets a hierarchy of appreciation, as opposed to watering down the aesthetic appeal. A tail that is bought serves just as much a purpose amongst fandom members as one that was custom-purchased or even hand-made; yet, an individually-crafted mask or set of claws is directly correlated to one's dedication to his or her fursona, which thus reflects his or her sincerity of involvement within the fandom. Traditional folk groups may suffer from industrialization as factories strip away the significance of effort to the masses (examples being mass-produced dream-catchers or Nordic pendants), but that is in part because of the lack of effort acknowledged of the mimicked model. Among furries though, even the industry-grade models are considered acceptable modes of expression, and it is from *that* acceptance that the incredible respect for hand-crafted or custom-made identifiers stems. Where the acknowledged folklore groups of much older societies relied on self-creation of identifying pieces, the industrial-era developing of the furry fandom allowed a coinciding of both market and homemade material; previous generations relied solely on their hands, and were therefore disregarded when mass-production of their symbols began. Given the comparatively contemporary nature as opposed to much older folk groups, it stands to reason that furries—as a developing subculture—utilize the methods available to them, inclusive of industry where previous folkloric societies developed exclusive of the practice.

Another prevalent practice within the subculture is that of costuming. Whether that be in the form of a small tail, ears, and fangs or the extreme of a complete fursuit of one's fursona, the nature of when and where these costumes are acceptable is very specific—of course one is able to wear garb outside of a convention or furry meeting, though the decision will most likely be met with quieted, discomforted observation by outsiders. During conventions however, these are available to be observed in abundance. Anyone who has a suit will inevitably showcase it, and those with tails and teeth will parade about just as proudly. The purpose of these is easy recognition in some cases, as the particular tail will show to others what species one's fursona may be, as do ears or horns. To some who wear suits, it can be a fun showcasing of one's character, and to others it may provide a unique form of detachment, in which they never identify who they are beneath the fur, thus allowing them to act differently than they may when in different company.

This appreciation of art is arguably a trait of all fandom members. Whether it is the making of one's own or the fascination at another's, artistic talent is admired as it bridges the gap between what people physically are, and what people identify as inwardly. Skill in artistic forms is deified within the fandom as it is the medium through which people can create the reality they wish to live; the fursonas they have created come to life before their eyes. Art is not merely an interesting talent among furries, it is how members portray themselves to others. The fandom is for many members

> [a] collection of people that all enjoy a similar interest in anthropomorphics, not [just] art but stories, religion, and all aspects of it including art as a costume or making a costume or anything like that…. It's not just fun, but also a good way for [people] to meet other people. (Shaw 2015)

A massive family of creativity and admiration for the extravagant collects through this extensive appreciation of art amongst furries. One can look at any picture another posts of his or her fursona and immediately relate with them in terms of sharing the fandom. Depending on the animal chosen one can guess traits; depending on the pose or clothes one can assume hobbies—art of a character permits people to portray themselves without ever saying a word, a particular form of introduction unique to the digital world. In recognizing the artistic, people appreciate each other, and this shared respect forms the basis for many relationships within the community, binding together through means that would otherwise not be expressed within an outsider group.

Despite its recent conception, the Furry fandom projects and maintains many of the qualities characteristic of the traditional folk group, including distinguishing linguistic deviations, group-specific methods of humor, garb utilized during particular social events, and—perhaps the most identifying step in the journey to becoming an individual entity—lack of knowledge on part of existing, outside groups. Whether it is an interest in art or the desire to fully express one's inner character, the furry subculture provides the means for a conglomeration of otherwise outsider individuals to congregate and befriend each other, all on the bizarrely specific basis of anthropomorphic identification. While media may portray the community as exclusively deviant, the reality is much more comfortable: it is an imaginative, friendly, fuzzy family.

REFERENCES

Brunvand, Jan Harold. 1998. *The Study of American Folklore: An Introduction*. New York: W. W. Norton & Company, Inc.

Chimera, R. [StormInAJar]. 2015. Personal communication.

Ebony (convention attendant). 2015. Personal interview.

Miko, J. [JulyMiko]. 2015. Personal interview.

National Geographic Channel. January 2012. "Secret Lives: Furries." *National Geographic Channel.*

The Neon Fox (convention attendant). 2015. Personal interview.

Raya [skullRaya]. 2015. Personal communication.

Reysen, Stephen. 2015. "Social Identity Perspective of the Furry Fandom." *Furries Among Us: Essays on Furries by the Most Prominent Members of the Fandom*. Nashville: Thurston Howl Publications.

Shaw (convention attendant). 2015. Personal interview.

Simo. [2009?] "The New Furry's Dictionary." *The New Furry's Dictionary.*

Zarroc [ZarrocBrisingr]. 2015. Personal communication.

FURRY EROTICA
Kyell Gold

Kyell Gold began writing furry fiction a long, long time ago. In the early days of the 21st century, he got up the courage to write some gay furry romance, first publishing his story "The Prisoner's Release" in Sofawolf Press's adult magazine Heat. *He has since won twelve Ursa Major Awards for his stories and novels, and his acclaimed novel* Out of Position *co-won the Rainbow Award for Best Gay Novel of 2009. His novel* Green Fairy *was nominated for inclusion in the ALA's "Over the Rainbow" list for 2012.*

He was not born in California, but now considers it his home. He loves to travel and dine out with his husband Kit Silver, and can be seen at furry conventions around the world. More information about him and his books is available at www.kyellgold.com.

One of the peculiarities of current furry fiction as compared to the mainstream is the ready availability of adult titles. In mainstream science fiction and fantasy, sex is hardly unknown, but it is softened, euphemized, and rarely mentioned in a book's description. Paolo Bacigalupi's *The Windup Girl*, winner of the Hugo and Nebula Awards, includes a graphic rape that in a furry book would certainly get it an "Adult" rating. You can buy it in any bookstore without being warned of that scene.

Furry books, by contrast, are segregated by both FurPlanet and Sofawolf into Adult and non. And while some of the Adult furry books are so explicit that they'd be classified as erotica by any publisher, many are not. For years, the primary furry marketplace was in-person at conventions, while SF and fantasy books were primarily sold through bookstores, which provided a level of distance for the books' publishers. At a furry convention, you would more than likely be buying a book from either the publisher or author directly. In the late nineties, as more and more young people joined the fandom, conventions laid down strict guidelines about selling and displaying adult material, so publishers tended to err on the side of caution when labeling.

As a result, any publication with even a single adult scene generally earns the label "Adult," and trying to figure out whether there is more adult material in the furry market than in the mainstream science fiction and fantasy market is a difficult exercise. But based on the classifications of the two major publishers, between 30 and 40% of the books for sale in furry fandom are Adult titles.

There's no secret to why sex is popular with any group of people. But why do furries continue to write about it and buy it? What makes furry a safe place for those books? And is there a deeper reason than just "sex sells?"

The connection between furry fandom and sex goes way back. At the core of it is probably furry fandom's conceit in which furries imagine an alternate body for themselves. Science fiction knows well that one of the first things people tend to be interested in when imagining a new body is, well, how does it have sex? While the very early days of furry fandom were not so sex-focused, at least not publicly, once the eighties hit, adult art became common, and on the Internet, adult writing began to appear.

The furry archive known as Yiffstar (now found at sofurry.com) became the largest repository of adult furry stories, with thousands by the mid-2000s. Most of the stories were along the lines of "what if this sexual situation happened?" but a few were more in-depth. The freedom and joy of exploration in these stories eventually made its way into larger, more complicated stories that explored relationships along with explicit descriptions of what people in relationships do.

And here's one of the interesting things: The proportion of gay and bisexual men in the fandom is greater than in the population as a whole (several surveys have shown this). In the nineties, gay relationships were vastly underrepresented even in science fiction and fantasy, let alone the more conservative mainstream. In furry fandom, they became the norm, and so here was one of the few places a young gay man could see positive representations of the kind of relationship he was interested in, let alone explorations of the different kinds of relationships gay couples have and a demystification of gay sex.

A word about that, because as noted above, furry erotica is often quite explicit. A lot of that is for the very obvious reason, but it's also important to note that part of the interest is curiosity: the stereotype of the SF fan with no practical sexual experience is something I personally have found untrue, but it is true that until recently, gay teenagers growing up could find porn (that's what the Internet is for), but couldn't find anything that integrated sex into their lives. If you want to see straight people having sex, you need only turn on any R-rated movie, pick up any bestselling book, turn on any of a number of cable channels. But gay romance, the path that leads from a spark to a date to more dates to an enduring relationship between two men or two women: that was more elusive.

As Yiffstar and other archives of free online stories grew,

the furry print publishing industry was just getting started. Early fanzines like *Yarf!* and *Pawprints* did well, but neither allowed adult content; other fanzines that attempted to focus on adult content generally lasted only one or two issues (this was not necessarily a statement on adult content, as most fanzines lasted three or fewer issues).

In 2002, Sofawolf Press debuted a magazine focused entirely on adult content, titled *Heat* (*Heat #1* contained a story of mine). Like their existing all-ages publication *Anthrolations*, each issue of *Heat* contained several short stories with illustrations; unlike *Anthrolations*, *Heat* included comics as well.

Illustrations have always been a large part of the art-dominated furry fandom, and comics as well. Phil Foglio's *XXXenophile*, dedicated to erotic fantasy stories that occasionally (well, more than occasionally) skewed furry, had done well, and as furries grew more confident in making their own comics, adult content naturally found its way in.

Sofawolf was at the forefront, but the DIY mentality of the furry community soon seized on self-publishing in its newer incarnation. Out were photocopied fanzines; in were comics printed through Print on Demand presses. Out were huge comb-bound manuscripts; in were Lulu and CreateSpace (online publications of novels continued, and continues to this day) with perfect-bound trade paperbacks that looked, if not fully professional, at least in the same family. The furry fandom could fill those books with whatever we wanted, and one of the things we wanted was sex.

This is around the time that my works enter the picture, and just as I feel an obligation not to focus too much on them, it would be disingenuous to leave them out. They have, after all, gone through many of the aforementioned stages: I gained a following posting short stories on Yiffstar; I sold stories to *Heat*; my work appeared in a Print on Demand anthology called *FANG*; Sofawolf Press published my first novel. *Volle* was (I believe) the first sexually explicit novel to win the Ursa Major Award, and I believe that its success and professional treatment from Sofawolf Press in many ways legitimized explicit fiction in the furry fandom.

Whether legitimization or imitation was the cause, more adult novels appeared in the following years. FurPlanet Productions, acquired by FuzzWolf in 2008, began selling a number of them, including Andres Cyanni Halden's *Hallowed Walls* series as one of the earliest and most popular.

As it became acceptable and common to write professional fiction with explicit sex over the last decade, that fiction has branched out into numerous directions. Fetish fiction has always thrived on the online repositories (just browse the tags on FA or SoFurry sometime), but published anthologies themed along fetishes are becoming common; comics often cater to one or more fetishes. This is part of what makes furry satisfying in a spiritual sense: it allows us to explore through fantasy subjects that interest us while keeping the dangerous (or apparently dangerous) parts of those fantasy lives at a distance until we feel more comfortable with them.

As I mentioned above with gay teenagers, people with interests in a fetish may feel lonely, bad about themselves, or frustrated, depending on how outré the fetish is. Furry is an open environment where if you can't find anyone who shares your interest in something, you can just write about it or draw it, or pay someone to draw it, and post it in the community. Chances are you'll find someone else who likes the same thing, and maybe some people who didn't know they liked it until they saw your art or read your story.

And you're unlikely to feel ashamed of your fetish once you spend an hour browsing furry community boards and see macrophilia, vorarephilia, microphilia, inflation, sneezing, tickling, watersports, and tentacles, not to mention furry-specific fetishes like paws and animal ears. Even if your specific fetish isn't represented (what are the odds?), it's clear that nobody is going to ostracize you for saying you have a thing for amputees or that you share Troy McClure's thing for fish. You can even fetishize sex with weird furless creatures if you want.

This open discourse in the fandom has generally (anecdotally) seemed to result in a place where people feel happier and more themselves. It's common to hear people talk about what they have to hide when they leave the realm of the fandom, whether online or at conventions (this is, by the way, common to science fiction and other fandoms as well).

At the same time as this broadening of fiction toward the erotic end was happening, the barrier between adult and non-adult fiction is also eroding. As late as the early 2000s, it was common to hear that your story could have sex or be a good story, but the two never went together. Early adult books, though they did include a plot and story and engaging characters, leaned very heavily on sex scenes (my own included). In recent years, though, we have seen a category of books emerge that include a few explicit scenes, maybe one or two over the course of a novel. Books are no longer marketed as "an adult novel with a great story!" but as "a great story (caution: contains some sex)." Rukis's works *Heretic* and *Off the Beaten Path* are good examples of this, and at least some of my recent books have followed the same path.

This is encouraging. The walling off of sex from the rest of storytelling, much like the walling off of sex from the rest of human experience, is not healthy, and here we see an acceptance that the occasional explicit sex scene may happen in a story where there is a sexual relationship (as it is important to the story). Sex includes moments of high vulnerability, often literally revealing oneself to a partner without disguise or artifice, and the writer can use those situations to reveal hidden layers to characters. Sex can also be fun and playful, and using it in those ways also removes some of the mystery and stigma from it. The way characters approach sex in one or two small segments of a larger story can flesh out their characters while at the same time reminding people that this is normal.

And however we reach that point, that is to me the primary benefit of erotic fiction (spiritually, at least; of course it has other very immediate benefits for some people): that it makes us comfortable with a part of our life that is often difficult to talk about. It helps us be open with our partners (or prospective partners) and understand our own desires and identity. And in this respect, furry fandom, which already has some very interesting questions of sexual desires and identity for some of its participants, is very much ahead of the mainstream.

THE HISTORY OF FURRY PUBLISHING
Fred Patten

Fred Patten (1940-current) has participated in the sci-fi/fantasy community since his joining the Los Angeles Science Fantasy Society in 1960. His writing credits include two books and thousands of reviews. He has also edited seven furry fiction anthologies as well as founded the Ursa Major Awards. Now, he is a member of the Furry Writers' Guild and the Furry Hall of Fame. He helped to co-found the Japanese anime fandom in 1977, receiving the Comic-Con's Inkpot Award. He now contributes reviews to Dogpatch Press and writes a weekly column on animation.

This is to some extent a "define your terms" question. Furry fandom got started, depending upon whom you ask, with the amateur press associations (APAs) *Vootie* and *Rowrbrazzle*. *Vootie*, "The Fanzine of the Funny Animal Liberation Front", run by Reed Waller & Ken Fletcher of Minneapolis s-f fandom, lasted from April 1976 to February 1983; 39 bi-monthly issues. *Vootie* self-destructed when its Official Editors, Waller & Fletcher, grew too disinterested to continue it any longer. A member, Marc Schirmeister of Los Angeles, tried to keep it going, failed, and started its replacement, the quarterly *Rowrbrazzle*, beginning in February 1984. *Rowrbrazzle* was designed so that, when the Official Editor steps down or is unable to continue, another member is selected to replace him. *Rowrbrazzle* is still going after thirty years; the current O.E. is William Earl Haskell of Houston, Texas. So it's technically a current furry publication.

Vootie and *Rowrbrazzle*, and later furry APAs such as the *Furry Press Network*, *Huzzah!*, and Canada's *FURthest North Crew*, exist(ed) as membership clubs averaging 25 to 30 members, whose members print their own fanzines in enough copies for all members, and send them all to the O.E. for assembly into a super-fanzine of 25 to 30 copies that are sent to each member. The only way to get a copy is to join the APA and publish your own pages. Private membership APAs are traditionally not counted as furry publishing.

The earliest generally available publication in furry fandom was the fanzine *FurVersion*, published by Kyim Granger (real name: Karl Maurer) of the San Francisco Bay area. *FurVersion* ran for twenty-one issues from May 1987 to November 1990. It began as a simple mailing list of furry fans' names and addresses, so they could keep in touch with each other in pre-Internet days. Fans began sending in their sketches and amateur fiction for publication, and *FurVersion* quickly turned into an amateur magazine for furry art & fiction. It had a cover price and subscription. *FurVersion* was the first of many amateur magazines published by furry fans from the late 1980s through the early 2000s. The most famous and successful was *Yarf!; the*

Journal of Applied Anthropomorphics, edited and published by Jeff Ferris of the San Francisco Bay area, with the help of Bay Area furry fandom. It lasted for 69 issues, from January 1990 to September 2003. *Yarf!* is currently being republished as five-issue volumes by Jarlidium Press of Seattle (see below).

Other notable furry fanzines were *PawPrints Fanzine*, edited by Conrad "Lynx" Wong & T. Jordan "Greywolf" Peacock; *FurryPhile Magazine*, edited by Brian L. Miller and later Bryon L. Havranek; *Steam Victorian*, edited by Zjonni Perchalski; *Mythagoras*, edited by Watts Martin & Bill Biersdorf; *Zoomorphica*, edited by Watts Martin; *FURtherance*, edited by Runé (Ray Rooney) of the Funny Animal Anti-Defamation League; *Gallery*, edited by Richard Chandler; *The Ever-Changing Palace*, edited by Lex Nakashima; *Fantastic Furry Stories*, edited by Mike Curtis; *Tales of the Tai-Pan Universe*, written, edited, & published by a furry writers' & artists' collective in Seattle; *Fang, Claw & Steel*, edited by Terry Wessner in Canada; *Fur Scene*, edited by Martin Dudman in England; *South Fur Lands*, edited by Jason Gaffney and later Bernard Doove in Australia. Kyim Granger ran Fauxpaw Productions/Publications from 1996 to 2006; two fanzine-format magazines, *Fur Plus* and *Fur Visions*, and several fanzine-format novellas, notably the *Fornax* series by Matt J. McCullar about the misadventures of four ratel sisters trying to become a hit quartet in the sleazy pop-music industry. A couple of these fanzines lasted for fifty issues or more; most lasted around ten issues; a couple lasted only one or two issues. *Tales of the Tai-Pan Universe* is the only one still being published, and it is a special case. It does not accept general submissions; all stories have to fit into and are carefully edited to fit into its fictional interstellar universe. (The *Tai-Pan* is a merchant spaceship with an anthropomorphic crew.)

These and other furry amateur magazines/fanzines ranged from home-mimeographed to professionally printed. In almost all cases, their editor was also their publisher. The individual publications disappeared for different reasons – in one case, a minor government official who did not believe in furry fandom threatened to have its editor arrested for fraud if he did not discontinue it, and the fan could not afford to fight it – but in general, in the early 2000s two things happened: (1) rising printing and postage costs meant that the publication would be sold at a loss unless the cover price and subscriptions increased so much that people would stop buying it; and (2) fan writers and artists switched to posting their works on Internet websites, and the free submissions of furry art & fiction that the publications relied upon dried up.

This did not matter too much, because by then, what most people mean by "furry publishing" had finally started. The first furry specialty publishing companies had appeared, usually getting their books printed through new print-on-demand technology. They had a rocky beginning, but by the early 2010s, several furry small presses were firmly established.

Furry fandom can thank Paul Kidd of Australia for this. Kidd has been a fanatic furry fan for decades. He submitted his earliest furry novels to mainstream publishers, who universally rejected them as too weird to sell. Kidd joined *Rowrbrazzle* in April 1989, and immediately started serializing one of his unsalable manuscripts; the furry 17th-century *Mus of Kerbridge*; so there is proof of when he started. Kidd did finally sell *Mus of Kerbridge*, published as a TSR Books paperback in April 1995.

The first furry book publishers began with Paul Kidd novels. Darrel Benvenuto, a grandiosely-promoting furry entrepreneur during the 1990s (he published four issues of *The American Journal of Anthropomorphics*, and advertised it as the leading furry professional magazine), announced around 1999 that he was starting the first furry professional publishing company. He did publish two trade paperback novels: Paul Kidd's unsold *A Whisper of Wings*, with a cover and illustrations by Terrie Smith (Vision Books, October 1999, vi + 348 pages), and the commissioned *The Rats of Acomar*, also with a cover and illustrations by Terrie Smith (Vision Novels, October 2000, 197 pages). *The Rats of Acomar* was written to be the first novel in Vision's *Tales of the Mornmist* series, and Benvenuto announced that the next three had been finished, each by a different author, but they were never published. Benvenuto launched a comic-book line slightly earlier, Vision Comics, with four titles. Most never got past the second issue.

Meanwhile, Martin Dudman started **United Publications** as a bookstore near London. United Publications was primarily a mail-order service for importing American books and fanzines, more comic books than furry titles, for sale to British fans. But Dudman did want to publish furry books that were high-quality that no mainstream publisher would buy. In April 2000 United Publications released Paul Kidd's furry Arabian Nights novel *Fangs of K'aath* (also serialized in *Rowrbrazzle* during the 1990s) as a hardbound book with a dust jacket and interior art by Monika Livingstone (iii + 364 pages). Furry fandom assumed that Kidd gave Dudman the manuscript for free just to get it printed. It was (and is; it's still available) a beautiful book.

Unfortunately, Dudman decided that publishing a "real book" was too much work. United Publications' next announced book was *Tales of Perissa* by Brock Hoagland; a collection of eleven furry pastiches of Robert E. Howard's *Conan the Barbarian* sword-&-sorcery adventures featuring a teenaged leopardess assassin. But when it was published in July 2001, it was little more than an 80-page comic-book format stiff-covered pamphlet of the first five stories. UP followed it up in January 2004 with *Tales of Perissa: Book 2*, also 80 pages with the six remaining stories; but only UP's publicity considered these "books". United Publications still exists, primarily as a British mail-order importer (a specialty today is American editions of Japanese anime & manga) but still publishing the occasional furry role-playing-game or furry comic-strip booklet. It does have three more "real" furry books to its credit: the novel *Fangs of K'aath II: Guardians of Light*, by Paul Kidd (January 2006, 337 pages); the collection *Tales of the Fur Side*, stories by Vixxy Fox, art by Dark Natasha (June 2006, 187 pages); and the hardcover *Sabrina Online: A Decade in Black and White*, by Eric W. Schwartz (April 2012, 164 pages). UP also publishes the annual trade paperback collections of the *Sabrina Online* Internet comic strip by Eric W. Schwartz; currently up to

#14. (https://www.up1.co.uk/)

United Publications is still going, but it publishes new books so infrequently that it is not usually considered as one of the successful publishers. Those are all in the U.S.

Sofawolf Press, founded by Tim Susman and Jeff Eddy and currently run by Jeff Eddy, originally from his homes in East Falmouth, Massachusetts and later St. Paul, Minnesota, and now from a warehouse in the latter, was the first really successful furry publishing company in the U.S. Sofawolf became official in October 1999 as a sole proprietorship, with its first publication, the furry general fiction magazine *Anthrolations* #1, in January 2000. *Anthrolations* was originally scheduled for semiannual publication in January and July, but it soon ran into the drying up of submissions – except for furry erotica, which Susman & Eddy did not accept for *Anthrolations*. #7 was published in July 2003, and #8, the final issue, was not until November 2006.

By then, Sofawolf Press was concentrating on trade paperback book publication and two annual magazines in booklet format, *New Fables* for general furry fiction and *Heat* for furry erotica. Sofawolf's first book (not counting *Technicolor Dreams*, the quickly o.p. two-volume collection in fanzine format of Will A. Sanborn's furry short stories, in January and June 2000) was the anthology *Breaking the Ice*, edited by Tim Susman (January 2002, ix + 206 pages), the first of his *Stories from New Tibet* series. Sofawolf's second book was *Best in Show: Fifteen Years of Outstanding Furry Fiction*, edited by Fred Patten (July 2003, 455 pages). That was an anthology of 26 stories advertised as the best from the whole range of furry fanzines from 1987 to 2001. Sofawolf's next books, like *Shadows in Snow*, edited by Tim Susman (January 2004), kept the publisher visible in the furry community, but it was with the publication of Kyell Gold's first novel, *Volle* (January 2005, viii + 317 pages), that the publisher really became prominent in the community. *Volle*, an X-rated novel featuring a homosexual anthropomorphic fox in the fantasy world of Argaea, won the Ursa Major Award for the Best Anthropomorphic Novel of 2005. Gold was the first furry author whose work was simultaneously graphically erotic and just as undeniably of high literary merit. Gold kept up his standing with his next books, *Pendant of Fortune* and *The Prisoner's Release and Other Stories*; just as erotic, just as high-quality, and published by Sofawolf Books.

At the same time, Sofawolf was establishing itself as a publisher of high-quality furry short fiction. The mostly-annual *Heat* series, an erotic magazine in perfect-bound booklet format, began in January 2004 but quickly moved to every June-July. There are eleven yearly issues to date. *New Fables*, Sofawolf's new title for non-erotic furry literature, is published less often, but there have been five volumes since Summer 2007.

In the last five to ten years, Sofawolf Press has added several new authors and artists to its list, including Kevin Frane, Ryan Campbell, Ursula Vernon, M. C. A. Hogarth, Michael Payne, and Leo Magna. Sofawolf is the publisher of Ursula Vernon's Hugo Award-winning six-volume *Digger*, and raised $140,000 through a Kickstarter campaign to publish a one-volume Omnibus edition. It can be counted upon to show up at several furry conventions a year, in the Dealer's Den with at least one table of furry books, calendars, T-shirts, the Artistic Visions artists' sketchbooks, and more; including at least a half-dozen new books per year. In Europe, it is represented by Black-Paw Productions of Germany and other furry specialty bookshops. By now there are over 75 Sofawolf Press publications. Sofawolf incorporated in March 2010 when its team had grown to four regulars, with Jeff Eddy as President and Treasurer, Alopex as Vice President and Secretary, and Tim Susman and Mark Brown as members of the Board of Directors. Sofawolf Press is not only the oldest of the major furry specialty presses; it is arguably the most prestigious of them. (https://www.sofawolf.com/)

FurPlanet Productions "snuck up" on furry fandom. The modern FurPlanet Productions dates from March 1, 2008, when current owner FuzzWolf in Dallas, Texas, bought it from FurNation's furry website founder, Nexxus. Nexxus started

FurNation in November 1996, and slowly expanded it into a major furry online community by the mid-2000s. FurPlanet was added in 2004 as FurNation's online store, and the publisher of the existing (since July 2000) *FurNation Magazine* plus some erotic furry comic books and novels. During 2006 FuzzWolf got involved with FurPlanet's publishing activities. His responsibilities grew, and he became the editor of *FurNation Magazine* with #8 in January 2007. FurPlanet also published the convention books for several furry conventions during 2006 and 2007. FuzzWolf and the rest of the FurNation group continued to grow apart, and during February 2008 he bought the FurPlanet name and its publishing activities, removing them from FurNation. (The magazine was returned to FurNation.)

Under FuzzWolf in Dallas, FurPlanet has continued printing furry convention books and erotic comic books. FurPlanet's first trade paperback book under FuzzWolf was the furry novel *When Summer Woke*, by David Hopkins (June 2008, 150 pages). FurPlanet mostly specialized at first in furry erotica, such as *Within Hallowed Walls*, by Andres Cyanni Halden (September 2008, 262 pages). It began to build up its non-erotic line with novels such as *Save the Day*, by D. J. Fahl (February 2010, 354 pages) and anthologies such as *The Ursa Major Awards Anthology*, edited by Fred Patten (June 2012, 341 pages).

Today FurPlanet Productions has a varied line of furry erotic and non-erotic novels and anthologies, erotic comic books, and "Cupcake" novellas. It has dealer's tables at at least a half-dozen furry conventions per year. In addition to its own publications, FurPlanet is also the distributor for Sofawolf Press at conventions that Sofawolf does not attend. (http://furplanet.com/shop/)

FurPlanet Productions actually has three imprints. The most prolific is FurPlanet Productions for those publications expected to sell mostly to the furry market. Argyll Productions is for those publications (mostly non-erotic) expected to have a wider, more general appeal. And then there is Bad Dog Books.

Bad Dog Books began in September 2005 as Osfer's Joint Publications, an independent specialty publisher run by Alex

Vance, an American furry fan living in Amsterdam; changing its name to Bad Dog Books in July 2006. Vance used Lulu.com as his first printer. Its first book was the short-story anthology *FANG, The Little Black Book of Furry Fiction*, edited by Vance. *FANG* specializes in furry gay erotica, often with a theme. Volume 1 featured stories in a contemporary setting; Volume 2, published for Halloween 2005, featured Halloween stories; Volume 3, featuring a fantasy theme, was released at Anthrocon 2007. When BDB began to get submissions of non-erotic stories, the publisher added *ROAR, The Little White Book of Furry Fiction*, edited by Ben Goodridge, in July 2007. That year, BDB formed a partnership with FurNation and its printing arm, FurPlanet, for its printing and distribution.

Bad Dog Books followed FurPlanet under FuzzWolf in leaving FurNation. By 2011, BDB had three volumes of *FANG*, three of *ROAR*, and several independent furry novels. But the difficulty in running an American specialty press from Amsterdam, plus Vance's longstanding health problems, resulted in the December 14, 2011 sale of BDB in its entirety to FurPlanet Productions. One of the terms of the sale was that FurPlanet would continue to publish the *FANG* and *ROAR* series under the BDB imprint. Today, there are five volumes each of *FANG* and *ROAR*. In June 2013, FurPlanet made Bad Dog Books its official digital downloads store; its website currently directs there. Bad Dog Books' past and present titles are regularly available on BDB's website, on FurPlanet's online catalogue, and on FurPlanet's sales tables at the furry conventions it attends. (http://baddogbooks.com/)

Rabbit Valley – Rabbit Valley Comics; Rabbit Valley Books; Rabbit Valley Inc.; Rabco Publishing Inc.; Another Rabco Disaster; Rabbit Valley Artists Cooperative Association – was started by Sean Rabbitt (two T's) in North Kingstown, Rhode Island in 1997; moving to Waltham, Massachusetts in 2001. He was joined by his partner (later husband) Andrew Rabbitt in 1999. There is a common misbelief that Rabbit Valley began in April 1987 as Mailbox Books, the first furry specialty mail-order store, by Ed Zolna of Roslyn,

Pennsylvania. Mailbox was a high-profile furry mail-order service throughout most of the 1990s. Zolna retired in Summer 1997, selling most of his business including the Mailbox Books name to Limelight Publishing Company, primarily an anime-fan specialty press in Honolulu, which resold it in April 1999 to Sean Rabbitt, who continued to operate both businesses during 1999-2001 until he was threatened with a lawsuit by a non-furry party over the Mailbox Books name. Rather than get involved in an expensive lawsuit, Rabbitt gave up the Mailbox name and consolidated both businesses under the Rabbit Valley name in October 2001. So it is not true that Rabbit Valley became just Mailbox Books renamed. (Zolna "unretired" in July 2003 and started Second Ed Mailorder, a similar furry mail-order service. It has a few titles only available elsewhere from Rabbit Valley, but does not publish anything of its own.)

Over the next decade, the Rabbit Valley Comic Shop expanded to add more staff and to offer mail-order sales of practically every furry publication that there was, including all books, comic books, and art folios. As Rabbit Valley Comics, the store published several furry erotic and non-erotic comic books of its own; notably the non-erotic *Circles*, begun in 1999. In April 2009, Rabbit Valley relocated to Las Vegas, Nevada. There were sporadic books earlier (notably the hardbound *Associated Student Bodies Yearbook*, by Lance Rund & Chris McKinley in June 2004), but the store's first regular furry book under its own name was an American edition in September 2011 of the 2006 British *Tales of the Fur Side* by Vixxy Fox and Dark Natasha, with a different cover. RV's first totally original trade paperback was *The Prince of Knaves*, by Alflor Aalto (March 2012, 406 pages). Rabbit Valley rapidly increased production until today it publishes several novels, collections, and anthologies a year, plus other furry specialty books. RV added a digital furry book distribution service in February 2013 that today has over a hundred titles available. RV is the publisher of the Furry Writers' Guild's first anthology, *Tales from the Guild: Music to Your Ears*, edited by AnthroAquatic (September 2014, 133 pages). RV also does DVD and CD manufacturing for the standup comedian 2, the Ranting Gryphon, and a half-dozen furry musicians. Rabbit Valley is one of the Big Three furry specialty presses (with Sofawolf Press and FurPlanet Productions) that attends numerous furry conventions a year; twenty-four during 2014, including four overseas. (https://www.rabbitvalley.com/)

Jarlidium Press was started by two Seattle furry fans, James "Tibo" Birdsall & Dan "Flinthoof" Canaan, in 1998 when they leased a commercial photocopier to publish fanzines, comic books, flyers, the convention books of Seattle's annual Conifur Northwest convention, and similar "ephemera", usually furry art-related. Over the years, occasional publications have matched professional trade paperback collections of newspaper comic strips, but these have been collections of Internet furry comic strips. The earliest of these was the *Dela the Hooda Treasury*, Volume 1, by Style Wager & Greg Older (June 2000, 118 pages). The most elaborate has been *Death on the Omnibus*, by Dan Canaan (December 2011, 339 pages), a complete collection of Canaan's *Roomies* anthropomorphic comic strip in a "real book" format. Beginning in December 2010, Jarlidium Press has begun a series of reprint collections of all 69 issues of the fanzine *Yarf!*, *The Complete Yarf!*, at five issues per volume. So far there have been three volumes: Volume 1, issues #0-#5, November 2010, 248 pages; Volume 2, #6-#10, November 2012, 248 pages; and Volume 3, #11-#15, December 2013, 290 pages; with Volume 4, #16-#20, scheduled for Further Confusion 2015 in January. The Jarlidium Press publications are usually available only by mail-order sale from Rabbit Valley and Second Ed, and the few furry conventions at which Birdsall & Canaan have a sales table. Jarlidium Press also took over publication of the semiannual magazine *North American Fur* with issue #4, Spring 1999; the current issue is #30, Summer 2014. (http://www.jarlidium.com/)

Anthropomorphic Dreams Publishing seems to be dead, or at least dormant, as a print publisher. It was started by Will A. Sanborn as WAS1 Productions, with trade paperback books printed through Lulu.com. Sanborn's first was *The Journey*, published in September 2007. His next five books were novels and collections by himself or anthologies that he edited, switching from WAS1 Productions to Anthropomorphic Dreams Publishing between his *New Technicolor Dreams* in November 2007 and *Alone in the Dark* in October 2008. ADP's first book by a different author was *Bait and Switch*, by Austen Crowder, in November 2010. ADP published a memorial collection of short fiction by Michael Bard, *A Horse of Many Colours*, in November 2011. Its last book was the novel *By Sword and Star*, by Renee Carter Hall, in February 2012. Since then, ADP has remained active through frequent audio podcasts, although there was a recent hiatus from December 2013 to June 2014, and nothing since then. It is unknown whether ADP will return to furry book publishing. (http://www.anthrodreams.com/)

Jaffa Books is Australia's first furry specialty press. It was founded in Brisbane, Queensland as a bookstore by Jacob F. R. Coates in March 2011, with its first books on sale in October; to import, publish and distribute both furry titles and authors with little to no publication history, especially in fantasy fiction. JB as an importer has become the official Australian retailer for FurPlanet Productions and Rabbit Valley, and all titles by Kyell Gold. Under the name of Jaffur Books, JB is consolidating all of its furry titles. Jaffa Books has been attending all furry conventions in Queensland (RivFur in Brisbane and FurDU in Gold Coast City) for the past couple years, and will expand to Western Australia (FurWAG in Perth) in 2015 and Victoria (ConFurgence in Melbourne) in 2016. JB's first original titles (only arguably furry) are the dragon fantasies *Axinstone* (December 2013, 252 pages) and *Impossible Magic* (August 2014, 235 pages); both by J. F. R. Coates in his *The Destiny of Dragons* series. It will publish its first "regular" furry novel, *Reborn* by J. F. R. Coates, in May 2015. (http://www.jaffabooks.net/)

That's about it. There are occasional furry books from other publishers – Mike & Carole Curtis' **Shanda Fantasy Arts**, primarily a furry comic-book publisher from June 1996 to

September 2012, issued two books; the cartoon-art *Here Comes a Candle*, by Mary Hanson-Roberts (July 2000, 215 pages), and the novel *The Iron Star*, by Brock Hoagland, illustrated by ten furry artists (July 2003, 160 pages). Two furry authors, both in Australia, have either started their own small presses or have self-published so many books that they seem like furry publishers. Bernard Doove in Melbourne has been writing on his website, *The Chakat's Den*, since 1995. In July 2005 he began collecting his short stories into books, at first through Kyim Granger's Fauxpaw Publications and then through Amazon's CreateSpace after Fauxpaw went out of business. Doove currently has 11 trade paperback novels and short story collections, available on Amazon. Paul Kidd in Perth started his **Kitsune Press** on March 2007 for his own books in paper and Kindle editions, plus those by other publishers, with printing of those not by mainstream publishers through Lulu.com. Kidd currently has over twenty books plus his role-playing games, comic books, and computer games available through his Kitsune Press website (http://paulkidd.net/kitsune-press/). Most of the books are also available on Amazon. Several other furry authors publish through CreateSpace and sell through Amazon, but with almost no exceptions, they have less than five books and use the CreateSpace imprint.

These, plus a few exceptions, are what is meant by "furry publishing".

YIFF? MURR?:
SEX IN THE FURRY FANDOM
Thurston Howl

Thurston Howl is the founder and editor-in-chief of Thurston Howl Publications. He is the author of the furry erotica book Where Carnivores Meet, *which received considerable media coverage in Nashville. His human-sona has also written a few books, namely* Farmost Star I See Tonight *and* The Sword of Destiny. *Howl is an avid reader and writer, and starts teaching his first course as Professor Thurston in the fall.*

Hello again! I told you that you would be hearing from me later on in this book (assuming you read the Introduction). For those who don't remember or didn't read the Introduction, the name's Howl. I am a folf dog (fox-wolf-dog hybrid), and I'm here to talk to you about sex! (This sounds like the most nightmarish way to start a sex ed class in high school. For that matter, furries and sex ed should just never mix.) So, many of you may know the term "furry" can hardly be spoken in public without someone assuming you're talking about a fetish. Furries are people who just like having sex in fursuits, right? I remember "coming out" as a furry[2] to a friend of mine, and he said, "Aren't those the suits with the holes in the crotch area?" That was a major face-palm (or face-paw) moment for me. Furries definitely have an unwarranted sexualized stigma in today's society. From my experience, the furry fandom has been about community, belonging, and just friends having a good time. However, there are certainly other aspects, such as art, fiction, music, fursuiting, conventions, and more. So, am I saying that sex is absolutely not a part of the fandom? Well, while sexuality is probably more important than sex in the fandom, I would (and do) argue that sex is a part of the fandom but not a *separate* aspect.

Let me start this by reiterating that the fandom's greatest value is its reliance on inclusion and community. No matter what your hobbies are, your favorite films, sports, books, or alcoholic beverages,[3] furries will accept you. This goes the same for sexual preferences. Whether you are gay, bi, straight, trans, pan, or anything outside and in-between, furries will be glad to have you around. As they are this accepting, they also are *open*[4]. Sex and sexuality are simply not taboo topics for furries. No,

---

[2] Since I've already come out of the closet as a gay man, can we call the furry's coming out "coming out of the kennel?" I think this idea has great potential, and I now lay copyright to it.

[3] For some reason, I still get looks when I'm drinking a mojito, and my colleagues are drinking beer. Mojitos are manly drinks, right?

[4] To those particularly witty furries trying to make a dirty joke here, stop.

this doesn't mean that furries meet at coffee shops and discuss their favorite sex toys, but it means that in private or online, most won't shy away from making sex jokes, sharing sex stories with close friends, or asking each other questions that their conservative high school sex ed never covered. They even have *some* unique sexual terms that further separate sex from the realm of taboo. Instead of the colloquial "fuck," furries say "yiff," supposedly being the sound foxes make when they have intercourse. "Murr" is another common sexual term that is a general sound of pleasure. One might use it in response to getting a back rub or the like. Also, furries tend to call their significant others "mates" as opposed to "boyfriend," "significant other," or the ever-abhorrent "bae." Note that none of these are terms for *new* ideas; they are simply animal variants of common sexual ideas. However, sex manifests itself in the furry fandom in more than just its lingo.

As Kyell Gold mentions in his article in this collection, furry literature does something that gay porn just doesn't: it enables for sex to be integral to a meaningful LGBT relationship, whether it is for young or mature audiences. College-aged furries can read about coming-out and sexual intimacy in the same novel now, something that can be notably harder to find in mainstream fiction. As he also notes, many furry novels have an Adult rating on them, even if they have just one adult scene, while many mainstream erotica novels do not have any kind of warning. With that said, one can see how sex, at least in furry literature, functions as an integral, or at least important, aspect of real-life relationships that mainstream literature usually does not capture in the same way.[5] Some sample authors of erotic furry fiction are Kyell Gold and Rukis. I feel no need to expound on furry erotica, as you could simply read Kyell Gold's article elsewhere in this collection.

---

[5] To clarify on this, I find that most mainstream novels either entirely skip the sex scenes while alluding to them, such as, "He led me to his bedroom, and I flicked the lights off," or more graphically describe the sex scene but through derogatory language, making it an unclean or taboo act.

Furry art is likewise open. On April 26, 2015, I searched FurAffinity (the main art archive for furries) for the word "fox."[6] Including NSFW (Not Suitable/Safe For Work) images, there were 667,477 results. When I shifted the toggle to Only SFW (Suitable/Safe for Work) images, there were 489,470 results. That means that roughly 73% of all fox images have a General or lightly Mature audience rating. There are several archives for furry art, including FurAffinity, e621, SoFurry, and various tumblrs. I feel absurd for quoting "The Rules of the Internet" here from 4chan (2007). Rule 34 states, "If it exists, there is porn of it." This is very true even for furries. From *The Lion King* erotic art to Mickey Mouse nude pictures, if you can name an anthropomorphic character, some artist has probably drawn it having sexual relations with another. However, from my experience, most furries look at this kind of art not as porn,[7] but with erotic appreciation. I have looked at furry art with friends, and it becomes a game of who can find the "hottest" art; it's not an intimate action. Many furries really do just admire the art. It is a sexually open fandom, and that openness plays into their art as well as their literature.

Now, let me address a myth I have definitely heard more than once. Myth #1: Furries like to have sex with animals. Absolutely not. The idea of furry is not "becoming an animal." It is about a completely new physical idea, the hybridization of human and animal. If such a creature was to exist, would it be ethical to have relations with it? I will not pretend to have the answer, and I acknowledge that many would be against it, but I also know that many would be perfectly okay with it as long as the being possesses human intelligence. Comparing furry to bestiality is akin to comparing homosexuality to bestiality: it just doesn't make sense. When a furry admires an erotic pose of a feline anthro character, they might say he has a cute tail. Maybe his human chest is very muscular. Maybe his clothes are so tight

---

[6] I chose to search for the word "fox" because foxes are simply awesome, and we're not narcissistic at all.

[7] I say this, but I'm sure there are those laughing, saying, "Yes, we do!"

that they reveal all his muscles, all his curves...I don't know if I was trying to be evocative just then, but I assure you I could do much better (and have done better, in my last furry work *Where Carnivores Meet*, #shamelessplug). While the furry fandom is sexually open, this doesn't mean that everyone in it *is* sexual. Even if a furry does "paw off"[8] to an erotic art piece, that does not signify the person wants to go into a barn and have intercourse with a horse.

Myth #2: Furries have sex in fursuits. This one is almost laughable. When I hear this, I ask them how much they think a fursuit costs. Usually, they might say two or three hundred dollars. Then, I have the pleasure of telling them it can be upward of two or three *thousand* dollars. Most furries aren't willing to cut holes in the fronts of their expensive suits for sex purposes. Fursuits are for social acting (see Keefur's article). Yes, there are furries who have sex in fursuits, but probably not more than people who have sex in space suits. Yes, fetishes exist, but the furry fandom is *not* a fetish.

With all of this said, there are two further aspects of furry sexuality I would like to discuss. One is stereotypes. Despite the fact that furries do not rely on sexuality, furries do apply sexual stereotypes to some people based on their furry identity, or fursona. For example, if someone is a fox, they are typically considered to be submissive, hypersexual, teasing, and on the receiving end. Wolves are usually dominant sexually. Bears (as is similar to the LGBT term) are larger in weight and usually hairier. Sometimes, the sexual stereotype is loosely based on existing folklore and/or mythology. With foxes being more cunning in fables, and with "foxy" being a word to describe a lusting female, a fox furry is definitely considered more sexual than others. Other times, as with bears, the fursona describes the body type stereotypically. Note however that exceptions abound. I have seen foxes who are "tops," bears who are skinny, and wolves who are submissive. Some furries actually

---

[8] The furry term for masturbation.

get annoyed when they are labeled by their stereotypes, though this is usually a mild annoyance. I would argue that when choosing one's fursona, it's important to also understand the cultural connotations for those animals inside the furry fandom.

For furries who are interested in anthropomorphic sex outside of art and actually wish they could explore anthropomorphic sex, there actually are options. There are fox tail butt plugs, werewolf dildos, and dragon penetrables. However, sites that sell these items usually label these products with names, such as "Rex the German Shepherd," "Chance the Stallion," and "Fenrir the Wolfdragon" (BadDragon website). These kinds of names personify the characters, separating them from animals, and bringing the toys back to "furry."

Overall, it should be easy to see how sex does exist as an element of the furry fandom, though it is far from an exclusive one. It is tied loosely to different aspects of the fandom. Art and novels don't *require* it; it is simply that the furry fandom is just so open with sexuality and sex that it is acceptable to discuss it freely.

MY EXPERIENCE WITH FURRY ONLINE DATING
Takaa

This is Takaa, just a simple panthion, or what most people would say a panther lion. He's 23, male, and gay, from Maryland, USA. Takaa has been in the fandom for about 3 years now. He started out as many other furs do: lurking. When he first started, he spent most his time on Pounced trying to make new friends. He went back into freelance writing about a year later, doing a few little pieces here and there. He then got into drawing. He uses an assortment of furry sites: SoFurry, Weasyl, FurAffinity, DeviantArt (not furry-exclusive). He's usually around FurAffinity though, since it's the simplest way to upload art and such.

I honestly don't even remember how I stumbled upon the fandom known as furries. I remember when I was still in high school; I was on DeviantArt looking at some inspiration for my mediocre writing. I figured "Alright, this is a nice-looking site – nice and clean." So I decided to look around the site and I saw the "anthro" category. I didn't know what anthro meant, but I looked and saw nothing but humanlike animals. I didn't know whether to be freaked out or amazed. I assume I was the latter since I kept looking into it. Eventually, DeviantArt led me to a more adult site called FurAffinity – well maybe not more adult, but less clean. Of course, my parents looming over me like hawks, I had to be careful what I looked at on that site. But it had tons of art, to extravagant to not-so-extravagant, and the clean to the not-so-clean. I figured I'd look more into this furry fandom.

Somehow, I made my way to the site called Pounced.org. You had to be 18 or older to join that site. So being the little nerd I was, I waited. Was it worth the wait? From my experience, I'd say 80% yes and 20% no. Like any other newcomer into a fandom or social group, I was eager to meet others that were into the fandom like I was. I navigated my way through to the forums and decided to introduce myself as Leon (my previous fursona). The people were friendly enough. Then I decided to finally make an ad there. I was eager to get replies. I got a few that were asking me if I wanted to hang out. It wasn't too hard to figure out what they wanted, but it was nice that they were subtle, compared to the other "you wanna yiff?" types that came along later. However, if I were to make some friends on there, I knew I'd have to be the one to break the ice. So I did; I messaged a few people (about a dozen). One or two actually replied. I didn't think there would be so many shy types or introverts there. I made one or two friends, though they didn't really last. Only one or two friendships actually lasted.

Facebook was another place where furries ran rampant. I learned more and more about the fandom. It wasn't that hard of a concept to grasp when I learned about it. I didn't even know it until I made a furry account along with my real one. As with the other sites, I poked around, looked at some groups, and saw some furry pages. One of those pages was Gay Furry Pride. This was where I found my first boyfriend (or mate). Something I've noticed is that I fall too quick and hard for people. When he broke up with me for someone that could visit him occasionally, it certainly hit me. However, I got back on my feet.

I decided to go on this site called FurryMate. It was basically like a Furry Facebook, though with a few issues here and there. Like for one, it had spam bots sending messages that looked like it was someone trying to talk to you. This was done to encourage you to subscribe. What tipped me off was when I got about ten messages in under a week. I'm nowhere near that interesting. Also, the unsubscribed users are very limited. We could send messages but can't read them. I tried to delete my account from that site, but I couldn't. Not sure if anyone else could. So basically they can keep sending me bot messages and I can't do much but just send them to spam. I'd rather have that spam not come at all, but I guess putting it in my junk mail is better than nothing.

Back to FurAffinity. Although it's mostly a site for people to post their art – furry related and non-furry related – I have made a few acquaintances on there, along with some roleplaying friends (the clean type). The good thing about friends on there is that there's little to no drama. The only issue is when you have those people that assume that this is a dating site. I can assure you it's not. The only ones that hook up on FurAffinity are the ones that are already dating.

Another thing I noticed that I'm not the only one that falls hard for people. On Facebook, lots of other furs do too. The only difference between me and many others is that I know when to back off. Others can be quite persistent. Some will even go as far as to send you on a guilt trip, talking about them being alone and never finding someone and how nobody will ever like their ugly hides, blah, blah. Some have even threatened suicide or harming themselves. If you have that much of an issue, then you need to see a therapist or a psychologist instead of worrying someone else.

First interaction with a fur on Pounced, FurAffinity, or even Facebook is quite different than just an average Joe; and no, I don't mean baby roos. I certainly don't mind the cutesy murring and purring and pawing (and I mean pawing at someone, not fapping); however some take the fursona thing a bit too far, acting like they're an actual wolf or fox. Sometimes they'll start sniffing my butt and I'll be sitting there like "Can I help you?" I know that's how animals act and all, but I'm not an animal; I am a furry, thank you.

In addition to the ones that don't think they're intruding on your virtual personal space, there are the ones that do it, and they don't mind. That's what they say – "I don't mind it. It's alright." Um okay, well do I get a say in who I want to touch me? Really if you're over 13, you have no excuse to be groping on someone or giving them a lustful hug without their permission, let alone continue to do it after they stop. Granted, I myself can be a bit horny and all, but I know when someone isn't feeling it, or they're uncomfortable with what I'm doing. Ever heard of "no means no"? Well that's what they mean.

I've pretty much stopped the online dating thing on Facebook. Why? Because too many people fell hard, and I fell hard for too many people. Also people cheat, or whatever one calls cheating these days. One day a couple is in super loving love, then they fall for someone else. Then they use the excuse that it isn't meant in the same way when a couple does it. How confusing is that? Then there's the jealous ones that always are stalking your conversations or looking at your messages. Note: never trust people enough to give them your password. It never ends well.

Also there's the matter of sharing pictures and videos and whatnot. Some see a "relationship" as simply sharing lewd or explicit pictures with each other to get each other off. Don't get me wrong; I have no issue with trading naughty pics, as I've done it countless times, however you shouldn't feel pressured to send a naughty pic, video or whatever. One thing I've noticed is that there are a lot of exhibitionist furries, who are basically furs that love to show themselves off. Hey, more power to you; thank you for sating my libido for a little while. However, there are some of them that decide to send a picture and expect pictures in return, as if there's a contract or something. If I didn't specifically say I would send you anything, don't expect me to send anything.

The only good relationships I've seen online are ones where the couple lives relatively close or with each other. Either that or they're introverted and they have very high confidence in the relationship. Some couples have so much confidence that they're in an "open relationship." The term varies greatly among the community. To some, it means whoring around without a care for your other; to others, it means a healthy means to keeping the relationship alive. To me, whatever works for you and your partner is fine. However, if you try to involve me into your little urges because you can't keep it in your pants while your guy or girl is away, please go away. Talk to your other and work it out, or break it off.

So to sum up, the furry fandom isn't much better for dating than with non-furries. Whether it's Match.com, FurryMate, OKCupid, even Facebook, take caution. Do some research; ask around; look at the About section if they have one. Dating takes time, and with the fandom, it takes patience. Trust me: people will certainly try your patience in the fandom. If you are trying to find a fur to be with, my suggestion is, like with any other relationship, take it slow. Don't rush, because that's how things end up getting messy...like sex.

WHAT DOES ART MEAN TO THE FURRY FANDOM?
Zambuka

Zambuka is a German shepherd from the antipodes. They've been active in the community since 2008, and have dabbled in a lot of different artistic pursuits including illustration, animation, fursuit creation, sculpting, and some writing. Since a wee pup, they've been getting paint on things, and drawing on things that are not supposed to be drawn on and generally thinking in unusual ways and having adventures of one sort or another. They have a fondness for tea, good coffee, animals, hiking, gardening, martial arts, dance, music, swimming, ice cream, creating, and investigating things.

Art is a large part of the furry fandom. Illustrations, writing, roleplays, costumes, sculptures, music, podcasts, comedy, dolls, plushies, and other assorted craft and hobby pieces are all a prevalent part of the fandom—something that has become synonymous with the fandom, and is what a lot of the online activity generated gets centered around. But why is it such a large and integral part, and why such a broad range of media? What does it mean to the fandom? How does it influence and change as the people in it change?

It's certainly a way to express one's self, one's ego. The options are almost limitless when one can choose from over 1.5 million described species on the planet. Add to that number the unlimited fantasy creatures and hybrids one can make and you have a lot of choice for what to use to perfectly express your personality: what appeals and what captivates. Often something will be picked that is readily identified with, so you'll often see dogs, cats, rabbits, wolves, tigers, horses, otters, parrots, and other animals that are often raised as pets or are wild and charismatic. That is what is familiar, interesting, and sometimes has some nostalgia. Then, there are hybrids which are mixes of two or more animals, or creatures that are plain fantasy (though sometimes have bits and pieces inspired by real world counterparts). Characters are anthropomorphic in some way. Usually a humanoid body with facial, hand, feet and tail features of the desired animal(s), but sometimes they're fully animalistic characters physically, but mentally are as conscious as humans.

There often seem to be phases of different breeds or species of animal that come to the fandom's attention, as well as the more frequently seen mainstays like wolves, foxes, dogs, cats, and dragons. The popularity of a breed or species can often be influenced by artists portraying them in artworks, and can often grow or fade depending on interest of other artists, or the response (or not) of the fandom in general. Anecdotally, some of the popular phases seem to have been otters, rabbits, sharks, deer, huskies, and German shepherds, all of which have persisted to one degree or another.

One of the reasons I personally chose a German shepherd over other dog breeds is that when I was quite young (I think 3-4ish) both of the neighbors that we interacted with frequently had German shepherds. I tended to pat and play with the dogs more than I spoke to the adults with their not terribly interesting adult talkings. I found them to be a very fun, energetic, and goofy breed, but also having a very gentle side (one that is often not represented in the media of guard breeds). So, I have a very early attachment to that breed specifically. I've tried on various other alternative characters, but none have so far fit as well in the fandom as the German shepherd. Others I've talked to have based their character off their favorite animal, off of animals they work with either as volunteers or a career, animals that have characteristics that they identify with, their spirituality (notably if they're therian or otherkin) or sometimes people will commission an artist to design a character they might like, or to buy a character that they can use as an avatar. Some people form close attachments to their characters, and others just use them as a representation in spaces where they can't see each other face to face, with a lot of middle ground that others will fall into.

Art can be a form of escapism into a character. It can be a way to overcome anxiety and act and express yourself in a way that you normally feel like you couldn't. When you're a character, you can be anything! From the most energetic socialite, to a king, to a cyborg or the cool loner, or secret agent. It can be a fantastic tool for people with chronic illness or disabilities, people who are trapped by circumstance, and simply a way to explore parts of your personality you may not otherwise get to engage. Even just taking a break from thinking about that boring meeting tomorrow and giving a way to unwind after work or school and relax is nothing to scoff at. Add onto that the genres that can be layered over that, sci-fi, fantasy, cyberpunk, film noir, and you have a recipe for an unlimited number of possibilities. Different medias can be used for different purposes. Illustrations for static scenes or badges, animation to add a little extra life and movement, writing for more detailed stories, graphic novels for shorter snippets that ask for visuals. Along with fursuits for the actors, dancers, and performers among us, and music to give us something to dance to! Each style of art has its own place depending on the desired effect or concept someone is trying to portray, and that varies with the wants of the individual creating it.

Art can also be a way to make an income. There are a lot of people who are willing to help support the artists in the fandom through purchasing commissions or through word of mouth (or journal or social media). One can take commissions to supplement rent or food, funding vet bills, and turning it into a career! There are a range of styles that various artists use, so you can find almost anything you want to represent your character from cartoony, realistic, stylized or something else entirely. Certain artists may specialize in certain sub genres, like cyborgs, high fantasy, steampunk, and some have a more general theme range, or are willing to take on a wide range of projects to stretch their artistic muscles and to get them out of their comfort zones. Artists are not always able or willing to take on new work, but there are enough open at any given time that art-o-holics can get their fill. Some artists will crowd fund certain projects, which opens up revenue for the artist that doesn't always involve commissions, as well as using donations either regular or one offs to fund certain projects or commission types. Most artists use social networking or dedicated art sites to conduct a lot of their business, some host raffles, and others will often stream their work so that other people can watch. How people offer commissions can vary a large deal: some do flat rates, some auctions, some as raffles through particular websites, and some charge by the hour. To add variation to that, you have commissions where the commissioner has total control, the artist has total control, though oftentimes it is somewhere more in-between. Sometimes premade scenes that you can get your character added to are offered, and sometimes premade character designs are available. Musicians and writers often need a little more information when crafting their work, but depending on the artist you choose, you can have as much or as little input as you like. It's a good idea to try and find an artist that meshes with your price and creative control requirements as well as style wants. Some artists are more oriented towards digital art, and some like to stick to traditional media. The popularity of digital art seems to have gone up, but traditional art is still valued as you actually get to hold the artwork in your hand.

But those aspects are all very independent. How does art affect the fandom on a more macro level? How does it build community and what does that community choose to do?

The easiest way to meet a large number of other furs in person is conventions. These will often have organized events, and quite frequently they have a lot of art-related events. These often come in the form of panels, which range broadly in topic (from how to draw wings, to fursuiting 101, writing, and music, to name a few). Also, art shows, where artists display original pieces or prints that have a chance of going up for auction if they get enough interest. It's a way that artists can get some extra income that is not commission-related. Often, conventions will have a dealer's den or artist's alley (or both!) where artists can sell merchandise, books, prints, originals, and sometimes commissions (often in the form of sketches to badges to be completed at the con, while others will take away homework to be completed later). Not to mention the often numerous dances and other music, acting or comedy-related events that are often planned for the evening events, which are often generously hosted for free by the people facilitating. There are often smaller art jams that will form, where artists can help motivate each other and offer critiques where desired (this also happens outside of the convention setting in some areas).

Conventions also offer another interesting opportunity. Oftentimes the con will hold a fundraising drive in the form of charity auctions, where artists will put up particular paintings, originals, prints, or other items or services in exchange for the fundraiser of choice for the convention. The charities money is raised for are usually animal-related, though not always. Some of the charities that have been fundraised for include Hello Bully (a charity for rescuing and rehoming pitbulls in the greater Pittsburgh area by Anthrocon 2012), Conservator's Center (a rescue, conservation, and education center for large and small cats, wolves, foxes, kinkajous, and more, located in Caswell Country, NC by Furry Weekend Atlanta 2007-2014), House Rabbit Society (a rescue and education center for rabbits in Richmond, CA by Further Confusion 2008 and 2011) and The C.A.R.E. Foundation (exotic animal rescue and education which includes big cats, bears, primates, alligators, and more located in Apopka, FL by Megaplex 2005 to 2014) among many more.

The largest charity auction amount raised so far seems to be Midwest Furfest 2012 with $40,500 raised in support of Felines and Canines (http://www.felinescanines.org/) who rescue abandoned, abused and neglected animals until their (hopefully) permanent forever homes can be found. They are no-kill, cage-free, and have been operating from Chicago since 1977, though they originally only rescued cats, and expanded to rescuing dogs as of 2012.

Art can be used as an identifier: it gives a way to bond with other people you otherwise may not have met, or even considered talking to. I have friends in the fandom with biology and geology degrees, animators, game developers, programmers, gardeners, janitors, retail assistants, and glaziers. There are people around from a lot of different countries: from the Americas, the Asiatic countries, Europe, Africa to the antipodes and almost anywhere else you could think of. Some have only just joined the fandom, and others have been around since the inception of the fandom as we know it today, having migrated from IRCs and MUCKs.

Some of them I would not have met without art, or other artists. I personally would not have even found furry without the art. Where else can one draw animal people and find other like minds? There is a very strong sense of community, and it frequently overlaps with other fandoms and interests. One of the most popular websites that tends to double as a social networking site and an art platform is Furaffinity. Some others are Weasyl, Inkbunny and SoFurry. Websites like these make it easier for people to congregate and find each other around a common interest. Other platforms that often get used are Facebook and Twitter, especially for general updates, and communication at conventions.

Art can also be a safe haven for members of the queer community. There is a large prevalence of gay, lesbian, and bi identifying people around, who are more openly, or very openly speaking and interacting. It is becoming more and more common that trans* artists are more sharing with their personal lives, including transitions they might be undertaking (both mentally and physically), which facilitates a broader understanding of the trans* and queer communities, as well as helping other individuals going through similar things to not feel so isolated, even if they might be offline or outside the fandom. There is also more awareness of different gender dynamics and how people choose to present themselves, as well as a broad range of attraction and romantic identities that are becoming more visible. Art gives a clear and easy way to show things that they would otherwise not have the option of clearly or easily presenting over the internet.

Art is an integral part of the fandom, working as a glue, a networking and expression tool that is rivaled by little else. Doing anything from comedy to fundraising to supplying income to artists, the fandom, and the artists that participate in it offer a unique way to express oneself and to meet new and interesting people one may not run across in the normal course of life. Art is a large and important part of the fandom in its various forms, and it looks like it'll stay that way for a while yet!

THE FUZZY NOTES OF FURRY FINGERS
Roo

Roo, (aka. Lucas Raymond), is a musician, music industry enthusiast, and geeky summer camp organizer. He has also moonlighted as a tour guide, cartoonist, coffee jockey, restauranteur, and small-town library page. Roo has a theatre degree from the University of Guelph where he has played a racist cop, a strung-out druggie, and many other wild people on stage. He also has a diploma from the Harris Institute in Recording Arts Management...a fancy way of saying "He learned the Music Industry." He has done everything from digital marketing for Universal Music, to running contests for indie artists, to co-managing an alt-country band, and now calls Dale Speaking - an indie artist promotions company - his home. An avid podcaster, he has hosted, co-hosted, or produced over 200 episodes since 2012. Since 2004, Roo has been chairman of Camp Feral, the furry fandom's oldest outdoor event, where he has inflicted his love of horror, low-budget films and the bizarre on hundreds of unsuspecting campers. He has a pink-mohawk, piercings and tattoos, and thinks he's a kangaroo with gargoyle wings, which is all perfectly normal.

In 2004, I traveled from Toronto to Philadelphia to attend my second Anthrocon. I was lucky. I had friends traveling with me. I also had a task to do: promote Camp Feral in the dealers' room during my first year as con chair.

But along with the t-shirts and flyers and grabbing a television at K-Mart so we could play footage from camp, I had an underlying ulterior motive. The table would not only be used to push a furry summer camp on unsuspecting prospective campers: I had also brought along fifty copies of my first solo album.

Long before I discovered the furry fandom, back in my rural Ontario...and internet-less...high school of the mid 90s, my primary outlet for creative expression was music. I had played piano since I was two, and was always obsessed with music and becoming a musician, but I didn't get to really live it until I formed my first high school band.

We were called the Overgrown Spatulas. We recorded off the cuff, semi-improvised songs of a subtly vulgar type, and we sold cassettes to our friends. Our first album, *One Day I Had A Cold*, sold fifty copies despite being grossly offensive, roughly recorded and badly marketed.

But the Spatulas eventually became Brillohead, a four-piece that took inspiration from our idols— R.E.M., Radiohead, Sloan—and actually performed live in Guelph, Hamilton, and at the legendary venues of Toronto: The Horseshoe Tavern, Lee's Palace and the meccas of all venues, El Mocambo.

I was the oddball of the group. I never chased any girls and had Disney pictures in my locker rather than pin-ups. I was always talking about cartoon animals. I would even walk the halls of high school with a plush Timon hanging out of my pocket, whom I regularly referred to as "my boyfriend."

I told everyone that I was half-kangaroo.

No one ever beat me up. I'll never understand why.

One of the band members was a cartoonist and artist with dreams of becoming an animator. I asked him one day to draw me as a bad-ass kangaroo with a machine gun belt around my chest, shouting a warning to all who would listen: Don't Fuck

With Roos.

I'd never heard of the furry fandom and wouldn't for another three years. Even when I discovered furry, it was actually after being a member of the were community, and only because a friend and I decided to go to FurryMuck to make fun of the "freaky furs."

Neither of us realized that it would completely change our lives. Sidenote: he's a furry now too.

Music and my interest in cartoon animals were always connected. I could never sneak animal references into the songs Brillohead played, but I did manage to write and record an entire song inspired by an image of Ayers Rock (Uluru) I had found in a book about Australia, a book I was reading to hopefully spy a picture or two of that weird beast whose connection I couldn't explain.

I also never found a way to admit that I was into guys. I say into guys because, until I was about to graduate, I always thought "gay" meant "a guy who dressed in women's clothes." All I knew was that people would set me up with girls and I'd turn into the goofy guy again. When we wrote songs about relationships, I let my best friend and co-songwriter write anything that mentioned a specific person, so I could tell myself I was singing his story, not mine.

University was the place that everything came together. By the end of my first month, I had found the weres. By the middle of the following year, I had gone full furry. And it took me less than a week to start realizing I didn't have to be weirded out about the strange thoughts in my head.

That happened thanks to furry, not the University.

I first found out about furries who made music through friends. There was Kurrell in Australia, and there was Wolf Note who would go on to bigger things when he left music behind and changed his name. By this point, I was fully immersed in my pursuit of a degree and a career in theatre, so my approach to musical creativity had changed. Now, I was trying to find unique ways to incorporate music into the plays I was directing.

Music never left. I just left music for a while.

Brillohead played our second show at the El Mocombo in 1997. We had all gone off to different schools but tried to keep in touch and practice when we could, since we were either commuting from or living close to Erin, our home town. The show was a big one. We had a lot of new material. We were really tight and comfortable on stage. I was in the zone.

There was an additional reason why I was so pumped for this show. It was the first time I was playing in my high school (now University) band in front of my newfound furry friends. I had come out to the band, awkwardly, a few months before. And I had been upfront about being a furry as well, which at the time wasn't a commonly understood fandom...especially among rural Ontario guys...but it wasn't a surprise considering my high school antics.

I had two furry friends there to watch the show—Silfur and Alex. At one point, Silfur and Alex—the gay and proud city boys—challenged Kevin and our high school friend John—two rugged country boys—to a game of pool.

Silfur and Alex won.

I will never forget this show. It was one of those defining milestones. After a great performance, we all went out front to talk about the show, and that's when the guys informed me that they had decided the band should break up. We were all moving to different cities. It would be too hard to practice and get together for shows. We had just played our last.

They hadn't told me because they knew I would be upset. They were right. When we parted ways, the three of them piled into a car with our equipment and drove home.

I went to hang out with the furs for the weekend.

The term "furry music" is a tough one for me. It's not just the semantics of it: what makes music furry? It's also the association people have with the term. When they hear "furry music" there's always a question about whether it's a genre, or a style, or are the lyrics all about animals?

When I started the Fuzzy Notes podcast in 2012, my goal was to give furry musicians a place to be showcased.

FurAffinity was the central hub for art. SoFurry helped writers. Musicians had groups, forums, webpages...but they were all text. You saw a picture of the music, and read the text of the music, before hearing the music. If you ever clicked play at all.

View counts, favourites and comments are also small potatoes compared to artists. The most popular musicians struggle to find an audience because the fandom is intrinsically visual- and story-based, which makes sense: the fandom was built on artists contributing to the culture, on writers contributing the culture, and the two combining to make comics and cartoons.

There was no Amateur Publishing Association for musical furs in the late 80s.

The SciFi crowd had a deeply embedded relationship with much thanks to Filk—the art of taking an existing song and altering the lyrics to suit the world, stories, and characters of their favourite TV shows, movies, and books. It was at once an homage to the culture that created their fandom, and a comedic way to expand on the world they lived in.

Furry has always been different. Apart from one or two exceptions, the furry fandom has created its own culture. The characters we grew up loving—from Albedo, or Falstaff, or in Circles—are created by furries for furries. For the most part, we don't turn to someone else's creation for guidance...we create the guidance ourselves.

You couldn't consume music as a furry the same way you could consume a comic book. So music never really had a home and couldn't create itself the same way the fandom did.

And I always wanted to hear what music made by furs would sound like.

In the early 2000s, the fandom wasn't devoid of music. Chris Goodwin has always been a cross-media inspiration, being an amazing artist, graphic designer, and musician. His MuleBoy albums were a breath of fresh air for a fur who wanted to find a musical idol who I'm sure helped inspire the rush of electronic music that still outnumbers other genres in the fandom.

"Electronica" or "Techno" songs with animal-themed titles were common. I would listen to them, and many of them were interesting, but I couldn't hear how they were "furry." It was kind of like the early days of discovering my furry inclinations before I knew what furry was. I ate the songs up and sought out anything that would be remotely animal-related, calling it "furry" whenever I found it.

Despite being a tight community in the late 90s, I know I missed a lot. There were probably a lot of furry songwriters uploading MP3s of their work to their website. It was just harder to find anything dedicated to furry music, so I had to rely on what I could find, or word of mouth.

In 2003, I started work on unloading the chaotic mess of disconnected songs bouncing around in my head. I had been jotting down ideas for years, but never took the time to record them. I had grown up in the era of the "Fostex 4-Track" and every attempt to dabble into digital recording ended in frustration.

My roommates at the time, Silfur and Verec, bought me a small Tascam portable 4-Track recorder. You put a cassette tape into it, and the head recorded your tracks in the same direction, so a two-sided stereo tape gave you four tracks to work with. By leaving one track open, you could record over the three tracks you'd laid down, magically freeing up three more tracks, though it meant the original three couldn't be touched, and over time everything could get muddy and out of sync.

Regardless, I used that machine to put down all the songs I needed out of my head. I was a furry making music, and I didn't know how many more there were of me. I assumed "furry music" meant "someone who writes songs about furs," and I knew that wasn't me. My furry side inspired the music, but it wasn't the music.

It was like high school all over again.

Once I had enough songs that I liked, we rented a better recorder and put down thirteen. My tendency to have my fursona drawn wearing a shirt bearing the name of a teen pop idol or gay icon...usually Tiffany, but Liza made her way on there once or twice...led to naming the album *One Man Boy Band*.

The music was as far from "boy band" as you could get. I wrote a song about a kangaroo disemboweling a dingo who killed his family. A love song about a dead raccoon at the side of the road. A cautionary tale about a man who wanted to become a fox and who was tied to a tree and burned for it.

Really pleasant stuff. But it was my stuff.

Verec had the audio skill...all I could do was put stuff down in a drunken fury, generally downing a bottle or two of Robert's Rock wine before locking myself in "The God Room"—a broom closet so small I couldn't stand sideways and hold my guitar, named that because previous tenants had scrawled scripture all over the wall in sharpie and pen.

Verec took the chaos and made it listenable.

And then I took the tracks, burned fifty CDs, and drove to Anthrocon.

There were so few furry musicians at the time that people tried to buy my CD impressed by the cover, thinking it was an art CD. It helped that Ferris had drawn the cover art. It didn't help that the only CDs being sold at AC in 2004 were actually meant to be thrown into a computer to see furry pictures.

It's funny to think that furry music was so rare that a CD in the dealers' room was for art, not sound. You would never make that assumption at a SciFi con or music conference. But at AC you had art, comics, books, and t-shirts.

Most people were confused at the table. I would give them headphones to listen, and they'd be treated to an opening track that didn't sound like anything on the radio, or anything a furry who called themselves a musician would write.

Disembowelling, wild dingoes. Kanga's on the rampage, headband, Rambo.

Live performance was more acceptable. That same year, I set up outside the Dealer's Den with an easel that read "Busking for Charity," a guitar and an open case. I'd play covers of popular songs in weird, folk-acoustic ways. I sang Britany Spears so people wouldn't run away, and when I had them captured I'd sing Sparklehorse or Radiohead.

When one person asked if I knew any songs about vore, I actually had a song to play them.

I woke up in a horse's stomach one foggy morning, his eyes were crazy as he smashed into the cemetery gate. And all I wanted was to be a happy man.

Sales were dismal. I didn't care. I had gone to a furry convention. I had sold a CD. I had played for a crowd.

There were furry bands. The most well-known I remember was Sub Level 3. I had bought their music without hearing a single note, I was just so excited that there were other people like me. When I played a show at Further Confusion 2005, I was sure they were in the audience watching. Though I might have imagined it.

I kept the furry music dream alive. I performed where I was accepted—Morphicon for two years, Anthrocon in 2006, every single Camp Feral I've attended, and later at Condition Furry, Furnal Equinox. I can probably claim to be the only furry musician to perform at a furry con in Brazil.

And I released more music. In 2005, I recorded and released the aptly named *ACEP*. The music was less chaotic, more serious, more pretty. In 2006, I collected music from my first bands—The Spatulas and Brillohead—and from my first two solo releases, along with some additional tracks I'd recorded in the previous year, and called it 'Scratch.' It was a 31 song compilation CD I sold for $5. I just wanted to spread the word that there were furry musicians with a catalogue of music, and there was plenty of room for more to follow suit.

I should stop here and note: I, in no way, believe I started anything with regards to the growth of furry music. And there has been a growth. I can't keep up with the new songs being uploaded to FurAffinity, on Soundcloud, being sent to my inbox for a feature on my furry music podcast. The music made by furs is prolific, multi-genre, and increasingly more professional and creative.

What I do believe I did was what all the other furry musicians at the time did. They felt like there was a need for a musical furry voice and tried to become one. Whether they cared (obsessed?) as much as I did about the state of music in furry, or the lack of other musical furs, or the absence of a central hub for furry musicians doesn't matter. They were making music. Because being a furry and being a musician are separate parts of our being. It's up to us whether we want to bring it together.

The more visible furry musicians have become, the more inspired furs are to become musicians.

I haven't even come near to the importance of FoxAmoore to furs who want to compose and mine the depths of orchestration and music theory.

I couldn't even assume that I have done anything like Bucktown Tiger has to bring hip hop into furry, and more importantly show that it's cool to write about being a furry and about the furry culture, while maintaining an unbreakable positive attitude about our community.

The incredible performance and skill of Matthew Ebel, who has created his own unique sound and story and practically made a fandom of itself.

The beautiful voice and amazing creativity of Colson, who has traversed so many genres effortlessly, someone who caught the ear of Reddit, and Gotye, and so many others with his songs. From theeverpresentmelancholy to Pacific//Hotline, it's hard to find a bad song.

The devoted fanbase and prolific catalogue of Renard Queenston. They have tapped into an aspect of fandom I couldn't even fathom.

Look Left and Pepper Coyote, one of the most talented songwriters the fandom has today.

So many talents. Casey Lalonde. Wolfgun. DJ Ear. Husky in Denial. Futret. Rchetype. Fevrier.

And the unsung talents: The Dead Pixel, theblackparrot, Berserker Shark, Scales, Jon Chatters, Silent Cicada, Hunter Coyote...I could name names forever.

In 2004, I was desperate to find other musicians who proudly identified as furs. I didn't know what "furry music" would sound like because it hadn't really been created yet. All I knew was that furry art was easily defined, and furry writing was the same. It was the creativity that inspired so many of us to become furs in the first place. That first time you read ASB, or saw a picture of Falstaff...replace that comic and character with the one who inspired you, and you know what I mean.

The early furry artists, and writers, and cartoonists contributed to furry and created our culture. They didn't do it for money. They did it for art. There were no fans...there were only other artists. And on the backs of that creativity we now have a community that spans the world, crosses cultures and languages, but means the same thing to all its members.

The furry musicians have done the same. It took some time, and some loneliness, but what musician doesn't spend time alone in their room honing their craft and seeking an audience.

I love what "furry music" is. Before I wouldn't know how to define it, because there wasn't enough of it to see what it looked like. But now there is.

Furry music is diverse. It is every genre, every style, every sound. Its lyrics are sometimes about animals, sometimes not. Sometimes, it refers to the life of a fur; sometimes, it refers to the life of the furry who wrote it.

Furry music can be played late at night at the convention dances packed with furs wanting to party until the early morning.

Furry music can be played on an acoustic guitar by a campfire or on a porch surrounded by friends.

It is sad. It is hopeful. It is angry. It is scared. It is ecstatic.

Furry music can be sung in English, in Russian, in Portuguese and in Afrikaans.

Its creators are tall and skinny, short and round, average, muscular, unable to stand for long periods of time because of health problems...

Furry musicians look as different from each other as their

fursonas do. They are sopranos, tenors, basses and struggling to hit notes.

They can pick up an instrument and play it on the first try, or they don't know diminished from augmented and let the computer handle that stuff.

Furry music looks like everything and everyone, is happy to be heard by anyone who will listen, and grateful when someone has something to say about it.

We were drawn to furry by the art and writing that created a window into the world of living, breathing anthropomorphic animals.

The music made by furs reflects that world and the people who live there. All the uniqueness and charm, the good and the bad.

FURSUITING AND THE FANDOM
Keefur

When Keefur discovered the Furry Fandom five years ago by chance, something inside him clicked, and he had found a home. A printer by trade, many furry conventions, authors, and artists have found a use for this greymuzzle from Memphis, Tennessee. He is something of a renaissance furry in that he has tried his hand at many of the talents that furries hold dear. His collaboration with Draconis, aka Calamity Cougar, has helped produce many funny Photoshopped parody posters that promote Fandom conventions and variety shows from coast to coast. He built his own fursuit, Cutter Cat the Sabertooth, (with some help from some friends), and has done writing in prose and song parody. He helps with the Furry Drama Show productions (and sometimes makes an appearance as Wilford Brimley to sell you Furabeetus supplies). He is also the president of FangCon, a furry convention headed for its third year in Knoxville, Tennessee. Outside of the furry world, he is recognized as an expert in dog behavior, trains dogs for various venues, appraises antiques as an avocation, and is the mascot for a cat rescue organization called The House of Mews. He has twice been a Guest of Honor at Mid-South Con as a pioneer in the sci-fi war game industry.

Hello, everyone. I'm Keefur, and this is my personal view of fursuiting based upon my own experiences as a fursuiter within the Fandom. I have a deep love and appreciation of this Furry Fandom of ours, and was most graciously asked to give my view. I am not a writer by trade, but I will give you my best attempt.

Let me first give you a brief background of myself so that you can gain a bit of insight into the origins of my perspectives and also to show you that I am pretty much a normal guy. I spent a great deal of my fifty-nine greymuzzle years as a carpenter and commercial/industrial roofer. I grew up in the family business and it was hot, dirty work. I did this for about twenty years, but I didn't realize what good conditioning it was for wearing hot fursuits. I retired from roof tops, did some stints as a commercial painter and worked in an aircraft composite shop. Again, I later found this to be excellent training for making fursuits. I also grew up in the fledgling years of the gaming world, and know many of the creators of the role play and table top games you play today, as I used to own a game shop on the side. (I even got to hang out some with Gary Gygax, the creator of Dungeons and Dragons.) This was my first exposure to the "strange and unusual" things in life. After I married in 1981, I got into dog training and showing. My credentials in the dog world are quite extensive, which I find quite amusing, because I fursuit as the mascot for a local cat rescue organization. I also worked as one of the founders of a St. Jude fundraising event for sixteen years. These organizational skills also have helped immensely in the creating/running of a Furry Convention. For the past ten years or so, I have been running my print shop. My avocation is antiques. It is something that I have done since I was eight years old, and I am used by the local public television station as an expert appraiser during their antique fair fundraisers. This is what I would probably be doing full time if I were not now a Furry. All that aside, what I consider my first real anthropomorphic "experience" was when I found myself unexplainably attracted to a drawing of a medieval anthropomorphic vixen character in the art gallery at a Gen Con gaming convention in 1975. I felt a strong kinship to this drawing, but alas, being a lad of only twenty years, I did not have the vision to start a Fandom based upon such things. It was only in 2009 that I discovered the Furry Fandom, and with a huge rush, a giant hole was filled in my life that I did not consciously know existed. Being Furry has now seeped into almost every nook and cranny of my life. I print extensively within the Fandom, I have fursuited for several years, and I have helped found a convention. For all those years I did not know of the fandom, I feel cheated, and how I found the fandom is a long funny story itself, but that is best told at another time. I felt it was important to let you all know a bit about myself before proceeding. Now for more interesting stuff.

When I'm in fursuit, things usually start like this. "Hi! I'm Cutter Cat the Sabertooth!" I act goofy, offer hugs, say some (hopefully) clever stuff and get my picture taken. This is when I'm usually asked questions by non-furries, such as "Why would you want to wear that costume?" and "What do you get out of it?" These are perfectly understandable questions posed by a curious public. I pondered my answer carefully. Why *would* anyone want to put on a twenty-pound fursuit with three inch fur, six inch fangs, and foot, hand, and head coverings that make it become so hot that living in the Mojave Desert would be a desirable alternative? It is very difficult to put a definition to emotions and feelings. Instead, I'll relate part of my answer in a couple of stories.

The first time I saw a fursuit, I knew that that was what I wanted to do. There was not a doubt in my mind. I hadn't been in the Fandom a week, and I knew my niche. I was enthralled by these costumed characters running around giving out free hugs and acting goofy. (If you know me personally, you know that acting goofy is not a big stretch.) I looked into the costs of getting a fursuit done. I saw that fursuits came in all different levels of quality and cost. Partials (head, hand/foot paws, and tail) started out at $300 to $1200 with full suits going for between $600 to $3000. I understand that a fur suit recently went for over $11,000! Well, being the frugal Sabertooth that I am, I decided to make my own suit and save money. I set my goals, drew up some concept art, and made a fursuit. I had friends sew up the parts I made, but essentially, I designed, cut, built, and furred up most of it myself. I had help from my friend, Wolfaya, who made sure I didn't design anything horribly wrong. I had spent hours upon hours on the internet doing research on how to build a fursuit. I ended up spending about $600 for my suit, and considering all the mistakes I made, I consider myself fortunate for doing it at that cost. My fur varied in price from $20 to $32 a yard, and I used the more expensive green foam that is supposed to last better. The head was built over a kick boxing head gear with teeth that I had a friend mold from teeth that were made from actual Sabertooth teeth. I had to take the teeth I ordered and use glazing putty to make them smooth before I had them remolded. It was a true labor of love, and the reason I picked a Sabertooth was because in real life, I was already a little long in the tooth (older).

I remember the first time I donned my fursuit. I was uncomfortable, hot, and it felt like I was going to fall over from a lack of coordination, but you know, I felt an almost electric rush when I put it on. It was in the parking lot of a Chinese restaurant with a group of Furry friends that I first donned my new suit in public. Everyone was looking, and I hoped, admiring it, when suddenly, literally 30 seconds after I had put it on, an Oriental lady and her husband came rushing up to me begging for a photo with them. Game over. I was hooked. Warning sign! I found out I was a camera whore!

Now for the second story. I live in Memphis, Tennessee, which is the home of the St. Jude Children's Hospital. I try to make myself available to visit with sick children whenever asked. Several years ago, I had a close friend ask me to come to a fund raiser for a little girl (who has since passed away). This little girl had an illness with a name so long I couldn't even begin to pronounce it. The point is, her disease was so rare and lethal, that there was no cure for it. My friend said that my being there in costume would really cheer this little girl up. At the time, I had never done a personal appearance outside of a convention, and although I doubted the good my appearance would do, I did agree to go. I showed up at the school auditorium at the proper time and found a secluded place to put on my suit. I walked in and found a group of perhaps fifty adults and one poor nine year old wheelchair bound girl. She could barely raise her head, but when she saw me, I could see her eyes light up as she struggled to move. Now, I choose to talk in fursuit, although the majority of performers prefer not to. I walked in, bypassed everyone in the room, and not giving so much as a side glance, went directly to this little girl and told her that I was there just to see her, and that I was going to give her as much attention, as many hugs, and take as many photos with her as she could stand. She was almost glowing with pride as she wordlessly managed to put her pale, shaking hand on top of my hand paw. I was glad I was wearing a costume head because I didn't want everyone to see that I was crying, knowing that this poor girl thought that meeting a fursuit performer was such an awesome thing in her tragic life. I took charge of her wheel chair and was her escort for the next couple of hours. Finally, having exhausted myself, I reluctantly had to go. She whispered to me and asked if I would come back. I told her all she had to do was ask. As I left my contact information with them, her tearful parents told me what a positive effect I had made on their daughter, and that it had been a long time since she had done so well both physically and mentally. It was probably the most humbling experience of my life. That was the moment that I realized what an enormous impact fursuit performing could have on others.

As I said before, the answer to the question of why I do it and what I get out of it is quite complicated. I cannot speak for all fursuiters, but as for myself, I would have to describe fursuiting as a form of giving. I suppose you could say that the reason I do it is to bask in the reflection of good feelings that I help create. What I get is whatever the person being entertained is willing to give back. It might be just a smile, or a wave, or it might be a huge hug and/or a photo opportunity. I consider them all gifts that cost nothing to the donor, but mean so much to me as an entertainer. If you are considering becoming a fursuiter, be warned! Fursuiting is highly addictive. You will find yourself craving the hugs and good feelings more and more. You will want art, badges, reference sheets, props, squeakers, silly hats, bandanas, and giant sun glasses. By the way, it also turns you into a camera whore.

When I am out of my fursuit, I am normally a very outgoing person, and I carry a lot of that into my fursuit performance. I am not as physically active as a lot of fursuiters because of my age, which is one reason I talk in fursuit. After all, having come from an Ice Age tar pit, Cutter Cat is promoted as the ten thousand year old Furry, right? He is so old, he only hunts in elevators so he doesn't have to chase his prey, so don't expect much of a jig out of him! I try to make up for the lack of physical prowess with a quick wit and a bad fox joke or two. I have also found that being in costume does provide a wall of anonymity that makes it possible to do things that you wouldn't dream of doing while not in costume. It also makes it possible to get away with many things a person out of suit would probably have to answer to the police for. *Looks to see if there is a squad car nearby* Once, while wearing my fine, feline Sabertooth fursuit, I went up to the main desk at a very posh hotel that was hosting the current Furry convention, and to the hotel staff, and in front of some non-furs, I loudly complained that I was, as a feline, very disappointed in their hotel because I had found absolutely *no rodents* at all in my room! The staff looked appalled at first, but then the meaning of the words soaked in, and then everyone just started laughing. Remaining in character, I just stomped off in a huff saying that there probably weren't any decent rodent dishes on the hotel menu either. Sometimes being loud and proud carries the day.

As a masked performer, you can always separate your real life person from your fursona by simply removing your costume. I can put that naughty Cutter Cat into a storage bin and become Keefur again with no harm done. If someone comes and asks me about something Cutter Cat has done, I just tell them to ask "him" about it when they see "him" I tell them "I'm" not responsible for what "he" does (wink, wink.) It is actually a common practice to separate the fursuit character from the real life person. I have talked to some fursuiters who claim that being in fursuit is a form of escapism for them. I do not feel so much escapism rather than feeling that it is a way of being "included." Suddenly, I'm everyone's best friend. I am not judged as a human, but accepted as a giant walking, talking stuffed animal, or perhaps even appreciated as a way for others to find escape from their own mundane worlds.

Most fursuiters enjoy the social interacting at conventions; hugging passerby, taking pictures, and sometimes staging small "episodes" in hallways to entertain others. Some fursuiters, I have found, really practice the art of performing, and the Fandom has its share of professional and semi-professional mascot performers. Then, there are those that push the envelope with their fursuiting and dance (really well) in fursuit. You need to be young, coordinated, and talented to do it. I take my hat off to those furs who entertain through the medium of dance. As the Fandom gains more fursuiters, these fursuiters look for ways to express themselves and give back to the Fandom. There are those who do photography and video work, which makes their experiences accessible to those who cannot get to conventions or do not have local groups to join. There are also those, like my friend, Draconis (aka Calamity Cougar with "The Furry Drama Show"), who entertain live, on stage for the enjoyment of the Fandom. I have a special spot in my heart for the dedication of Furries who give of themselves to try to make the Fandom a better place.

Another question I often get asked is "Why doesn't everyone wear a fursuit?" Well, fursuiting, as I have said before, is not for the faint of heart. It is hot, and physically demanding. Vision can be a problem, and some suits require handlers to help keep their wearers safe. A suit is very confining, which brings the whole claustrophobia thing into play, and cost is also an inhibitor. Wow! Fursuits can be really expensive! To some

Furries, it is the art, music, or companionship that fulfills their needs. Needless to say, not all Furries will wear a fursuit. I don't think less of them for this, because one of the joys of the Fandom is its diversity.

As a printer, I am exposed to many different types of fandoms. Want to start an argument with a bunch of Trekkies? Just ask them which captain was better, Kirk or Picard? Go to an anime con and you will see attendees cosplaying and arguing with other different cosplayers as to whose anime is better. There is no internal cohesion within most Fandoms. With furries, it is the exact opposite. As an example, once, at Furry Weekend Atlanta, about a hundred and twenty-five fursuiters left the convention and went to Momo Con, an anime convention that was being held very close by. There was a long line of fursuiters wending their way down a busy downtown Atlanta avenue en route to our destination. We went as a "flash mob" that suddenly showed up at their convention en masse. Once we got to the heart of the Momo Con convention space, we stopped and howled. That's it. Then we left. We had a good laugh and everyone had fun in both fandoms. Later, we had lots of the anime people show up at our hotel. I questioned one of them about why they had come over to the Furry con and got an astounding answer. She said that Furries knew how to have fun. Furries got along, enjoyed each other's company, and had great costumes and costumers. She said that Furries "got it right" as far as being a Fandom.

Now, I will be the first to admit that my reasons for fursuiting are not universal to all Furries. I am not here to sway, convince, or otherwise cajole you into believing as I do. I am just one Furry, doing what Furries love to do, and that is to have fun. I can state the obvious, and say that fursuiters are the most visible facet of the Fandom. If you lined up a hundred people in regular clothes and said pick out the Furry, you would be at a loss, but put one of them in a fursuit? ...'nuff said. I do believe that fursuiters are a critical catalytic agent within the Fandom. They are the special glue that holds the Fandom together. The Fandom is a unique environment, and by unique,

I mean that they are both diverse and cohesive. It is with a sense of pride that I say that I am a fursuiter in "*That* Fandom... You know... the one that dresses like *animals*?!!" Fursuiters are ambassadors of good will to the entire world. They show us what we can be if we stop taking ourselves so seriously and just have fun without strings attached. They are walking advertisements that say "Furry is Cool!", and that Furries are comfortable with who they are. It is fursuiting's innate cuteness that draws the attention and sometimes gets non-Furry people to stop and ask themselves that one big question all Furries have already asked themselves, "If I like this, am I a Furry, too?"

FIRST FURRY CONVENTION AT CALIFUR, 2008, A MEMOIR
Corvin Dallas

Corvin Dallas is a 34 year old male blue jay from the greater Los Angeles County that holds a bachelor's degree in video game design and works in the video game industry. He has an immense love of video games, engages in drawing or graphic design in his spare time, and is a nerd bird. Been a lifelong furry as far back as he can remember before even learning what the word furry meant and continues to find camaraderie in the fandom. His original fursona was a tiger but it was later changed into a bird to better reflect his changed outlook on life.

Corvin has been attending furry conventions regularly since 2008 and has owned a fursuit since 2013. He works to contribute to the furry community in a number of ways but not limited to hosting panels at conventions, participating in dance competitions, and 'acting like a bird'. He tries his best to set a good example and showcase the good things that the furry fandom has accomplished. Corvin can be reached on Twitter @CorvinBirdy and is happy to share his knowledge and experience on the fandom.

When I was approached with an offer to write about Furry Conventions, I figured why not? Been to *counts fingers* twenty, twenty-one furry conventions so far. So I might be able to share some insight into what it's like to attend one, and hopefully dispel a few of those inaccurate depictions from mainstream media's reporting of furries that has thus far, largely been journalistic sensationalism along the lines of a click-bait article title like "Ten terrible secrets furries don't want you to know about furry conventions!"

But before we barrel full speed ahead, an abbreviated introduction about me. For simplicity's sake, my current "fursona" slash alter-ego is a blue jay named Corvin Dallas. Corvin's first name was homage to blue jays being part of the corvid family, and Dallas as a tongue-in-beak reference to the movie, *5ᵗʰ Element*. Corvin is a fursuit that I got back in July 2013, but I have been attending furry conventions as far back as May 2008. You can find pictures of Corvin on Twitter @CorvinBirdy.

People chose to attend furry conventions for various reasons. For me, the decision to attend my first furry convention was a combination of curiosity from being a self-identified furry over the last decade when I first discovered that "furries" was a word on the internet and was in the proximity of the venue where I lived in the eastern Los Angeles County area. My internal logic was such that if the whole thing was a bust, I would have only wasted a ticket and a couple gallons of gas to drive there. And thus, I set out for Califur 2008, held on May 15-18, 2008 at the Hyatt Regency in Irvine, California as an attendee, the cheapest membership level available.

Let me tell you, it was intimidating attending an event where you don't know anyone there, nobody, nada, zip, zilch. I remembered waiting in the registration line with a gentleman standing behind me with a demeanor that was "squirrely" (not in the furry kind of way), muttering to themselves, while pacing in a circle. Up until that point I had never met another furry in person and that first experience was almost enough to get me to press the eject button and head on home. Thankfully, I decided that one person behind me in line was not indicative of everyone else. After going through registration, the experience of seeing my first fursuit in person was magical. It's like having only seen birds in pictures and then seeing the real thing in front of you for the first time. They were fluffy, cute, and watching the fursuit spring to life was taking it to a whole other level. There were hugs, lots of hugs, more hugs, and photos taken.

Saw people walking around the convention with great-looking badges of their fursonas. A fursona is a furry character that anyone can create for any number of reasons. It can run the gamut of representing someone's inner spirit animal or guide, to an alter ego, all the way down to a fashion statement, or something just for fun. Being that a picture is worth a thousand words, it's easier to simply show a picture of an anthropomorphic tiger than it is to describe one. A badge is a shorthand representation to other fellow con-goers your character and mine sucked because I made it myself and was an artist with modest artistic talent at the time.

Have no fear, at furry conventions they have everything you need to fit right in. There was a modest selection of artists that I could have picked from in the artist's alley. A crash course of what an artist alley is, it's a less formal version of the dealer's den. The dealer's den is space the convention has formally set aside to sell stuff, requires an application, pre-planning, and generally don't allow last minute walk-ins or arrivals. The artist's alley or its equivalent by contrast isn't always but usually is in less formal space, but is more accommodating for people that either couldn't find space in the dealer's den because it filled up, or if somebody suddenly decided that they wanted to set up shop. Since I didn't really know any of the artists there, I simply went for one that had a green long-eared gryphon as their avatar, Likeshine. After commissioning her for a deluxe full body badge I resumed my adventures at the convention.

Up until this point, I was keeping myself busy with wonderment admiring fursuits which was fine and dandy, but as the convention wore on, I found that I still didn't know anyone. Being much shyer than my current self did not help matters any. Having some minor artistic talent, I opted to check out the creator's lounge. The name may vary at other furry conventions. But the basic premise is that it's a room usually filled with tables, chairs, open for most hours of the convention, and was designed for attendees to sit and art jam together. Found an empty table, took out my drawing supplies and started drawing.

As people came by, if they seemed friendly I'd try to strike up a conversation with them and go through a script designed to be an ice breaker.

"Hi there, how you doing? See that table over there?" I'd point to the table full of people.

"That's the cool kids table. This table is not as cool as that, but it's still cooler than that one." I'd point to an empty table.

That's usually enough to elicit a few chuckles and get the stranger to sit down and start chatting. Yay! Didn't make any lasting friends in the creator's lounge, but it was a fun way to pass time drawing, exchanging gift art, and chatting with strangers that share a common interest in the furry fandom.

That brings us to the fursuit parade. The fursuit parade is the cornerstone of all furry conventions. It's where everyone gets together to celebrate and admire fursuits, one of the most visible icons of the furry fandom. There's a set route and people can sometimes stake out good spots well in advance. Being a newbie, I got an okay spot about 15 minutes before the parade started. The procession of fursuiters began. I gawked at and got to see all manners of species and combinations thereof, differing costume styles from realistic to the cartoony, and it's just plain cool to see that many fursuits in one go.

At the end of the parade, I followed the procession to where they gathered all the fursuits in the parade to pose for a group photo. Managed to work up the courage to talk to Orzel, the only bird I found from the parade. (What can I say; birds are rare, and I have a slight bias toward birds). Asked for permission to take a picture with him in the Tern costume, and it made my day.

The rest of the Califur convention consisted of attending a panel or two but nothing that was overly memorable. Overall, my first convention was low key, and I met only a small handful of people. But it was my step that set me off to seek out more conventions. It started the process of helping me come out of my shell and become a more outgoing person.

My time at furry conventions was mainly taken up by drawing at creator's lounges at first, given that I didn't know that many people, with small amounts of socializing and attending panels. As I got more comfortable and got to know more people, that ratio started to shift toward more socializing and less time spent sitting around drawing. Ever since I got my fursuit in mid-2013, things have taken a dramatic shift toward fursuiting with some time socializing, but haven't had time to sit around to draw any more. I do miss drawing at conventions, a bittersweet progress of sorts.

A strange phenomenon I've noticed at conventions were how social interactions like making new friends or spending time with old one feels like it's running on accelerated time. Most conventions last a weekend but it feels like I've spent an entire week getting to know them. This means friendships can blossom rapidly over the course of a weekend. It also meant that the convention ending can feel like running into an emotional brick wall when you realize everything was about to end and return to "normal."

I'll close out with a crash course on what to do if you find yourself attending a furry convention for the first time. If you are a furry and already know friends that are in attendance, meeting up with them at the conventions can be a blast and have fun hanging out. Side notes for those outside the fandom that want to attend a furry convention to indulge in your curiosity, understand that things are not as weird as the media may make us out to be. It's not a secret society or club. It's a group of people hanging out that share a common interest. That's all. Oh, and bring a camera. You'll want to take pictures if it's your first convention.

A giant heads-up. You do not need to own a fursuit to attend a furry convention. By and large, the vast majority of people attending do not have a fursuit. Going off attendance and numbers from fursuit parades,[9] you're looking at roughly 12-32% of the people having a fursuit at the most.

Those that want to make friends, try attending panels. All furry conventions offer a variety of panels covering a wide range of interests and topics. Panels are great for finding people that share a common interest and hang out after the panel is over. Introduce yourself, exchange names, and make a new acquaintance!

Those into partying should look for nightly dances and depending on the convention, there may be a party floor. Conventions with a party floor are where people throw open room parties and loud noises are generally tolerated on designated party nights. Personally, I prefer something less chaotic, but that option is there.

Those into art and drawing can find kindred artists at the creator's lounge. Enjoy jamming out with fellow furries drawing art, possibly taking part in an art exchange, and doodling in someone's sketchbook for fun. I've had good times and memories in there.

There are also general events. The ones not to miss are, of course, the fursuit parade and possibly fursuit games. Most conventions also have a sort of variety show on one of the nights. The variety show is a talent show of sorts where you can see furries from around the fandom showcase music, song, dance, skits, and more. Speaking of talent, if you want to see people in fursuits putting on moves that you wish you had, don't miss the dance competition. The dealer's den and artist alley is the place to go for an art commission or souvenir. Those with a little more money can try their hands in the art

---

[9] **Convention attendance numbers (WikiFur):**
Califur 10 — 12%
Biggest Little Fur Con 2 — 32%
FurtherConfusion 2015 — 18%

auction.

I've traveled all over the country and met lots of people and made many friends at furry conventions over the years. They offer a place where people can put who they were on hold for a weekend and come together to celebrate a common interest. It's a break from the daily routine where bills and deadlines are replaced with parties and fursuiters.

Currently, I'm continuing to attend many furry conventions, primarily on the West Coast. Further Confusion, Califur, Rainfurrest, and Biggest Little Fur Con are just a few and thinking of expanding to those on the East Coast. Travel cost is one of the factors that's keeping me from attending even more of them. Instead of attending panels, I find myself volunteering to run them. Instead of watching the fursuit parades, I am in them. I am looking to give back to the furry community, and this essay is one of those ways I try to give back to the community that has given so much joy to me. Hope you enjoyed reading this, and go forth, be fuzzy, and have fun!

FURCONS:
THE INS AND OUTS
Zantal Scalie

Although he's been involved in the furry fandom for five years, Zantal the crocodile is still young in his time as a published author. His first short story was published in an anthology in 2015; this is only his second piece of published furry-related literature. As you'll see, he's been involved in many other facets of the furry world—from art to friendships to amateur writing to fursuiting/costuming. Each new event and interaction has brought new fun and meaning, and he continues to explore the rich world that is the furry fandom.

These explorations represent a variety of interests and activities—and a lot of Zantal's free time, most notably spent at conventions, fursuiting in public (from events to subways to concerts to airports), socializing, and wishing he had more time to write. He also loves combining interests: finding the furry theme park enthusiasts, car racers, "furtographers", and skiiers.

While Zantal owns 3 full fursuits and 3 partials, and he has many more ideas in mind for the future, the crocodile character will always be the most fitting. He's the one that feels the most right, and whose "fursonality" closely matches Zantal's own—just with some inhibitions removed.

Everyone remembers their first time. You start out nervous—you've heard a lot about it, and seen plenty of videos of it, but the real thing is bound to be different. You've looked forward to it maybe even for years, and you've heard stories of escapades from friends. When you finally get your first chance, you shyly rush into it and are soon swept away by the feelings, the world of new experiences. It's like you hadn't lived before, as if you really know yourself better now. It's over before you want it to be, but you know you'll do it again as soon as you can.

Furry conventions, or furcons (not to be confused with *the* FurCon, FURther CONfusion, in CA), can be a transformative experience (literally) for those in the fandom. It's a coming of age almost—someone's first convention often marks the beginning of a journey that melds their furry enthusiasm, their furry life, with their real one. For some, it is near the beginning of their entry in the fandom; for others, years are spent on the sidelines before jumping in. But whatever stage someone is at when they attend their first, it is certain that they won't forget it.

First times are often pretty similar. Not knowing very many people, new furs will tend to hang around a small group of friends. Each person they know, though, will introduce them to another six, eight, ten new people. Inclusiveness, friendliness, and welcoming attitudes abound; it seems like everyone was just waiting for them to get there and take them in. Seasoned furs become guides for this strange wilderness, showing newcomers the highlights—opening ceremonies, dealer's den, the art show, the guests of honor, the fursuit parade, the dances, the common areas, the room parties—until finally the whirlwind is over. A bit shell-shocked, but filled with wonder and memories, new furs leave with a larger group of friends than they ever expected and a longing desire to do it all again.

I'll never forget my first furcon. Unlike some, I arrived alone. I'd only lived in Seattle for a few months, and I knew hardly any furries in real life. Stepping out of the car and heading toward the hotel, I saw it, and I stopped in my tracks.

A fursuiter. A *real* fursuiter. One that I could approach and touch and maybe even hug, and I might be able to talk to him, only I didn't know what was acceptable and what wasn't…

Suddenly, I realized how little I knew about fursuits (or conventions), no matter how many pictures I'd seen. Was it okay to run up to them? To try and talk? How would they react? Did they all know each other? How many would there be?

I didn't try anything, for now. I could meet my friends and ask them. They've done this before. They should know.

I found the friend I knew the most, and the rest of the time was spent at his side getting used to this entirely new atmosphere. People wearing tails, people selling art, people discussing in panels, and most of all, people socializing with their other furry friends…it was all so new and so interesting.

The open, inclusive, and welcoming nature of the fandom was clear even from this first day. I'd planned to just make a day trip of it, but my friend insisted I stay in his hotel room. I'm glad I did; sometimes there just isn't a substitute for the bonding done late at night over pizza and cheap but tasty mixed drinks.

Day 2 was much of the same. A lot of firsts—first time commissioning artwork in person, first time hugging a fursuiter, first time introducing myself by my furry name…first time commissioning adult artwork in person. That last one was so awkward, trying for the first time to describe things that had been taboo, not-to-be-said aloud. Somehow it didn't click for me that since she'd done art like this before, it's not like the subject matter would scare her. She'd heard it all before; nothing I would say would be even mildly surprising for her.

It's funny to remember how things that seem so familiar now seemed so foreign then. Character badges, for example— I'd never needed nor seen one before, but when meeting a lot of new furs, it was really nice to have names (and animals) on display to put with faces. They're out own version of "Hi, my name is _____", but much less silly-feeling.

It was also striking, melding the online world of fictional

characters with the real one. Furs I'd gotten to know as fierce dragons or adorable otters were now brought to life as humble humans. Muscular, big bad wolves revealed themselves to be young, short, and shy, or petite and effeminate creatures to be tall and lanky boys in real life. But, while their appearance might not match their character, the personalities were every bit as interesting and varied as the physical characters are online.

My energy levels stayed high throughout the day. I love variety, novelty, and being social, and there were so many new things to take in and people to talk to. It seemed like there were endless new stories to hear—character backstories, personal backstories, hobbies, fandom observations…never before had I been exposed to such a wide cross-section of society. There are furs from basically all walks of life, with all sorts of jobs and interests—from retail employees to rocket scientists, and from millionaires to high schoolers.

Before I knew it, another day was wrapping up, and it was time to head home. There is perhaps no bigger endorsement to the fun of the con experience than what follows—Post-Con Depression, or PCD. Newcomers may not experience it their first time, but it's so common amongst those with experience that it's commonly referred to, and parties will be held the following weekend to try and combat it.

But, there are plenty of fun things in life that don't come with sadness when they're finished. What is it about furcons that makes this so acute? My theory is that PCD is particularly common because for many furs, furcons are the one place they can really let loose and not feel any stigma or worries. For others, it's a 72-hour party with many of their best friends, some of whom they won't see again for several months. Or, for other furs, these conventions are the only place they have a chance to practice their hobbies. Sometimes it's all of the above and even more. Considered in this light, it's easy to see why leaving it can be so hard.

This then leads to the obvious next step—going to another furcon. It's fascinating, too, to watch how furcon experiences change over time. How I spent my time at my first furcon is drastically different from how I spent my time at my last furcon. Furcon experiences are incredibly varied. The different ways each furry spends their time, and what they associate with most strongly, are almost as diverse as their species and characters. Let's look at my own experience to see how different con experiences can be, even from one person's experiences.

Before I start, I want to point out that you cannot do everything at a furcon. It's impossible, and even doing all the things I *really* want to do has gotten harder as I've grown more attached to the fandom. Simply put, I enjoy more things and have more friends in the fandom now than ever before (and hopefully this is true for most people; I like to believe the fandom only grows better with time).

Second, it's easy to think from the outside that furcons are mainly about fursuiting/costuming. After all, that's the most visually striking part of a convention, the part that conventions themselves often try to publicize, and the part that most non-furry media covers (yes, we are often a newsworthy event, it seems). But I didn't have a fursuit or really get involved in that until I'd been to several conventions. That was perhaps my most drastic shift in my interaction with the fandom, but we'll get to that.

As I mentioned, my first furcon, I spent most of my time following around my friends and socializing. I went to a few panels to see what they were about, and I commissioned some art. Panels, honestly, can be some of the most underappreciated aspects of conventions. Few of my friends go to any panels, probably just because there is so much else to do. But, I still attend a few, because it's an amazing chance to get insight into artists' creative processes, to see the guests of honor, to learn something new, or to meet people with shared interests.

One of my favorite panels, for example, features a fursuit maker who now makes incredibly detailed costumes for Hollywood. He now only really participates in the fandom through his close friends and these once-a-year panels, so it's one of the few chances to see him. Other panels are great chances to get tutorials on writing, acting, fursuit sculpting, drawing, realistic coloring/shading, or any other creative art. For me, some of the most fun is when I find panels presented by artists I've heard of and like.

Another place to find some talented artists is the dealer's den. Shopping can be a surprisingly large portion of some furs' convention goals and experiences. Though furry art, products, etc. are easily available online all year round, some artists only do commissions at a con. That may seem strange, but it's a chance for them to do quick sketches within a set timeframe. If they were available to commission for sketches online, some of them would be very overwhelmed, so they only take them at conventions. The most popular artists will have a line as soon as the dealer's den opens, and they may even sell out of their available time slots for commissioned sketches within the first half hour.

Of course, commissioned art is far from the only product in the den—or in the artists' alley, or in the art show. Stuffed animals, soap, furry comics, books, sculptures, and even complete fursuits can be found. Some of my most memorable purchases from my cons include a chalk-art, wall-sized triptych of a dragon (which even my non-furry family thought was cool) and some fursuit parts from a professional costuming company that had just happened to hear of the convention and decided to try it out. I've not missed an art show yet.

Those three focuses—social, art, and panels—continued to be the majority of what I did at cons for my first few furcons. But I continued to develop as a fur, and how I spent my time continued to shift. It's actually pretty striking how differently I spend my furcons now than I did four years (and eighteen conventions…) ago. The two things that made the biggest difference were meeting more furs and getting a fursuit.

Conventions bring together geographically disparate furs. For some friends, this can be my only chance to see them for the next few months, or even the next year. It's also a great, safe environment to meet people you previously met online (whether they are friends, artists, fursuit makers, or something else). I've gotten to the point where I make a quick list of people each con so I don't accidentally forget or miss anyone—furcons can get very chaotic with everything going on, and it can be easy to let something (or someone) fall through the cracks.

As I've continued going to furcons, this has become a larger part of how I spent my time. Of course, it can also be combined with other activities—attending the fursuit talent show, hanging out with some artist friends who are working on commissions, etc. Anthrocon, the biggest furcon, has an area they affectionately call the "zoo," which is just a bunch of tables in a room—a sort of "empty canvas" social space. It has become one of the most active areas of the entire con. This really shows the value of a wonderfully casual space to do art / play games / meet up before dinner / chat / just interact.

Room parties are also a part of the social fabric of a convention. I didn't attend any of these my first few times, and indeed, they're entirely optional. They also run the gamut from wild to tame, from ones that are basically a casual board game night to ones that could put fraternity parties to shame. I still don't spend a ton of time at these, but if my friends host one, or I'm up late and in fursuit, they can make a very entertaining diversion.

Fursuits, in particular, have been one of the biggest shifts in how I spend my time, because they've become one of my biggest passions in the fandom. I could probably write entire chapters on the different aspects of fursuiting—how I found out about them, what it was like to get my first one, the commissioning/character design process, the emotional attachment to them, acting and becoming that character, signs that you might be a fursuiter...fursuiting is one of my biggest passions in life, one of the things that excites me most. It may not be for everyone, but it certainly clicks well for me.

I digress a bit, though. This isn't about my fursuit addiction: it's about furcons. Whatever a particular furry's passion, furcons have something for them. In my case, it rapidly became fursuiting. In addition to art shows, I've also never missed a fursuit parade at a convention. Initially, I was in the audience, shooting pictures (photography is another of my hobbies). Two years after I attended my first convention, I received my first fursuit. It made its first appearance at the same convention that I started with, and since then, it's been an ever-increasing part of my life.

Although I probably won't do this again, at the last furcon I went to, I spent time in eleven different fursuits. Fursuiting around was basically my entire convention, with some breaks for a couple panels, the art show, and socializing. It was a really good time, but it also took away time from the other things at the convention (and it kept me from seeing everyone that I wanted to). With all of the fun opportunities available, you actually have to start thinking about how you want to prioritize things.

There really are a lot of things you can do just in fursuit, too. Walking around, seeing friends, and doing the parade are some of the most classic things to do. Some fursuiters dance; others compete; others perform at the talent show (which takes different names at almost every convention). Then there's public suiting, like going out to eat or out to a bar near the convention center.

Trading fursuits can be extremely fun, too, and that's how I managed to get to be so many different characters. The suit owner gets to enjoy seeing his character and interacting with it—hugging, talking, playing, etc.—and the other fur gets the chance to become a character they've never been before. I used to act in school and community theater, too, so it's probably understandable that I love jumping into another character's head and getting to act them out, even if that character is a big fluffy animal.

Fursuiting opened one other door for me, as well—dancing. Not in the sense of dance competitions, but in the sense of the nightly dances that are held at furcons. While I did go to the dances before I had a fursuit, I don't think I ever really truly let loose until I was in suit—the concept that fursuits enable people to have more courage and lower inhibitions is a fairly common one. For some, it's that they feel more attractive; for others, it's just that they feel more comfortable as their fursuit, but it always seems to increase self-confidence and help people relax. For me, once I had a fursuit, I let the music carry me away. I love dancing in fursuit, and I'll usually attend most dances at a con.

While my most recent con may have been a little extreme, I have spent a significant portion of my recent conventions in fursuit, especially in the evening. Even just walking around as one of my or someone else's characters is a blast, and that accounts for at least a couple of multi-hour blocks each day.

All of this is just speaking from my own experience, too. There are aspects of the fandom that I haven't even really experienced—such as the dance competitions, fursuit sports, and gaming. There are also some special events, such as jazz concerts, murder mysteries, or comedy shows, that not every furry convention has. The amount of diversity is really amazing, which is perhaps what bring such a wide range of people to the fandom—there are so many ways to fit in and express your creativity.

Furry conventions. To someone who's never been, it may seem strange that we go to multiple conventions, year after year, but if they, too, understood the variety of ways they offer to express ourselves and the friendships we experience, they'd be just as addicted as we are. Being in an entire building full of welcoming people with shared interests—and all the big, friendly, fuzzy animals—is the cat's meow (and the dog's woof, the wolf's howl, the crow's caw, the alligator's bellow, the dragon's roar...). Furry is a passion that connects to other passions, that encourages so many ways of being creative, and cons are the human embodiment of that.

There's no end in sight for me. I couldn't be happier. I hope I'll see you at one in the future.

THE ORIGINS OF THE INTERNATIONAL
ANTHROPOMORPHIC RESEARCH PROJECT
Raphael Dogustuc – Kathleen C. Gerbasi, Ph.D.

I am a Social Psychologist, Anthrozoologist and Psychology Professor at Niagara County Community College. I have been interested in furries for over a decade and I am the original peer-reviewed furry researcher. I am also a "dog person". Our children are all grown and my husband and I have four shaggy canine family members, all having come to us from various rescue organizations.

Since purchasing the basic elements of a fursuit at the Anthrocon Art Auction a few years ago, I have developed a fursona and a furry name, Raphael Dogustus. My furry name was partially derived from the names of some of Ivan Pavlov's dogs. The look of my fursona is a tribute to one of my dogs, Sparky, who has crossed the Rainbow Bridge. He was a springer spaniel/basset hound mix and I created the long ears of my fursona in tribute to him! It has been a joy and privilege to be associated with the furry fandom for these many years. I am honored to have made so many furry friends.

Kathleen C. Gerbasi 1
Courtney N. Plante 2
Stephen Reysen 3
Sharon E. Roberts 2

1 Niagara County Community College
2 Renison University College, University of Waterloo
3 Texas A&M University-Commerce

Author Note

This research was supported by the Social Sciences and Humanities Research Council of Canada. Address correspondence to Kathleen C. Gerbasi, Department of Psychology, Niagara County Community College, Sanborn, NY 14132. E-mail: **kgerbasi@niagaracc.suny.edu**

Anthrozoology is defined as the study of the relationships or interactions between humans and other species of animals. As a social psychologist, I was already academically focused on the scientific study of how humans think about, influence and relate to each other, so given my life-long interest in all species of animals, it seemed like a natural path for me to make the leap into Anthrozoology. When I first learned about furries, early in the 21st century, I realized there was no scientific, peer-reviewed studies about furries, and that the furry phenomenon seemed to be a fascinating blend of many species of animals, including humans, and thus relevant to anthrozoology.

In 2005 I had a furry in one of my classes and he expressed an interest in attending Anthrocon, which for 2006 was located in Pittsburgh, a convenient four-hour car ride away. I received permission from Anthrocon Chair, Dr. Samuel Conway, also known in the furry fandom as Uncle Kage, to send a research team to Anthrocon in 2006. We received IRB approval through Kent State due to the collaboration of my biologist/anthrozoologist friend Dr. Penny Bernstein.

In the following year, I submitted a poster on the original furry study to the Society for Research in Identity Formation

(SRIF) (Gerbasi et al., 2007) and also offered a panel discussion on the topic (Gerbasi, Harris & Jorgensen, 2007). Uncle Kage put me in touch with some highly regarded furries who lived in the area where the conference was being held. So I met with Karl Jorgensen and Brian Harris, who not only participated in the panel discussion at SRIF, but they generously gave me much wonderful advice on how to get more people to participate at future Anthrocons.

In the summer of 2007, I attended Anthrocon to conduct a follow-up study and submitted *Furries A to Z*, (Gerbasi et al 2008) the first ever published peer-reviewed, empirical research article on furries.

In 2010 as a result of the ongoing research, I was invited to give speak at the very first Furnal Equinox in Toronto, Canada. After I completed my presentation, one person said, "My friend has to meet you, he wants to study furries too!" That connection began the collaboration with Courtney "Nuka" Plante, which was really the beginning of the International Anthropomorphic Research Project (IARP). Nuka's enthusiasm, academic background, and furry identity were essential in the formation of IARP.

Our desire to use a fandom measure (Reysen & Branscombe, 2010) in 2010 lead to our collaboration with Dr. Stephen Reysen. Since we had used his measure, and because of his interest in various fandoms, Dr. Reysen began conducting studies at Furry Fiesta 2011, and the IARP has had a presence there ever since. Dr. Reysen's impeccable scholarship has contributed in countless ways to the growth and success of the IARP.

While a graduate student at University of Waterloo, Nuka proctored an exam for Dr. Sharon Roberts, and she became the IARP team sociologist. In 2012, she attended her first Anthrocon, and has been contributing a sociological perspective to our research. Not only has the IARP benefitted from her keen sociological insight, but through her dogged persistence and hard work, she earned the team actual grant money to help fund our projects. She has also assumed the responsibility for research projects at Oklacon.

In addition to the following student who have assisted with various furry research projects: Charlie Aquilina, Ashley Borelli, Eric Broeker, Troz Brueghel, Mike Cline, Carlos Darby, Emma Verratti DeChellis, James Ducas, Erika Edwards, Caitlin Fulle, Tim Gadawski, Anthony Hartman, Rebecca Hewitt, Justin Higner, Dan Kish, Elise Koepke, Darryl Lockie, Jared McCaffrey, Brian Mendel, Nick Paolone, Anthony Paterno, Adam Privitera, Tristan Puffer, Jennifer Raymond, Isaia Sciabarrasi, Joe Vullo. Special thanks go to the thousands of furry participants, to Laurence "Green Reaper" Parry, William Conde, Michael Brenner and Douglas Muth (Giza) for their continued support and interest in furry research, to and Simona Ghai for her amazing transcription abilities.

References

Gerbasi, K. C., Paolone, N., Higner, J., Scaletta, L. L., Bernstein, P. L., Conway, S., & Privitera, A. (2008). Furries from A to Z (anthropomorphism to zoomorphism). Society & Animals: Journal Of HumanAnimal Studies, 16(3), 197-222. doi:10.1163/156853008X323376

Gerbasi, K.C., Paolone, N., Higner, J., Scaletta,L.L. Privitera,A., Bernstein, P., and Conway, S. The Furry Identity: Species Identity Disorder (?). Poster presented at Society for Research on Identity Formation, March 2007, Sterling, VA.

Gerbasi, K. C., Harris, Brian & Jorgensen, Karl. Furries: Why do some humans grow up wanting to assume a non-human identity? Interactive Session at Society for Research on Identity Formation March 25, 2007, Washington, D.C.

Reysen, S., & Branscombe, N. R. (2010). Fanship and fandom: Comparisons between sport and nonsport fans. Journal of Sport Behavior, 33(2), 176-193.

"BY THE NUMBERS":
COMPARING FURRIES AND RELATED FANDOMS
Nuka – Courtney Plante, Ph.D.

Dr. Courtney Plante is a social psychologist and co-founder of the International Anthropomorphic Research Project, a group of social scientists studying the furry fandom. He began identifying as a furry in 2007, when a friend introduced him to a local gathering of furries, which he began attending weekly. While he formally identified as a furry in 2007, his interest in furry dates back to the late 90s, when he was an avid admirer of furry webcomics and furry-themed chatrooms. His fursona, Nuka, is a neon-blue cat in a lab coat who loves science and marshmallows and who, more often than not, ends up on fire as a result of an experiment gone wrong. Dr. Plante usually attends several furry conventions a year, where he studies furries, gives talks to furries about the IARP's research findings, and fursuits as Nuka. His current research interests include the psychology of fantasy engagement and immersion into fantasy-themed worlds. His current furry interests include watching his favorite artists via livestreams, learning to draw furry characters, and watching My Little Pony: Friendship is Magic. *His favorite ponies are Vinyl Scratch and Twilight Sparkle.*

Courtney N. Plante 1
Sharon E. Roberts 1
Stephen Reysen 2
Kathleen C. Gerbasi 3

1 Renison University College, University of Waterloo
2 Texas A&M University-Commerce
3 Niagara County Community College

Author Note
This research was supported by the Social Sciences and Humanities Research Council of Canada. Address correspondence to Courtney Plante, Department of Social Development Studies, Renison University College – University of Waterloo, Waterloo, Ontario, CANADA, N2L 3G4. E-mail: **cplante@uwaterloo.ca**

When I (Nuka) went to my first local meet-up of furries almost eight years ago, I can vividly recall having two distinct thoughts: "Wow, for the first time, I'm in a room full of people who share my strange interest," and "who exactly are these people?"

Who Cares About Numbers and Statistics?
When I joined the furry fandom, there was almost no credible, systematically-collected data about furries. Despite this, furries and non-furries alike made claims about the furry fandom. Television shows, talk shows, and newspaper articles, regularly made inaccurate, unsubstantiated claims about furries (e.g., McMahon, 2009; Gurley, 2001; Zuiker et al., 2003), while furries themselves routinely argued about issues in the fandom

(e.g., sexuality and the "Burned Furs"[10] movement, "Burned Furs", n.d.). In the absence of reliable data, less-valid forms of evidence, including anecdotes and stereotypes, inform opinions (Shermer, 2002, p. 48-61). Scientists, however, recognize that the plural of anecdote is not data, and rely on neither intuitions nor stereotypes, which can often be incorrect.

In response to the lack of reliable information about the furry fandom, several social scientists and I formed the International Anthropomorphic Research Project (IARP), a multidisciplinary team seeking to scientifically study the furry fandom. The purpose of this research is two-fold: on the one hand, furry research has proven to be a valuable way to test, and in many instances extend, existing psychological theories on fan communities, fantasy, identity, human-animal relationships, minority groups, and stigmatization. On the other hand, furry research can also dispel inaccurate stereotypes about furries and help both new and lifelong furries to better understand their fandom.

Where Do These Numbers Come From?

There is no perfect way to collect data (Plante, 2014). The strengths of any one study are undermined by its inherent weaknesses. For example: surveys allow researchers to investigate the interaction of dozens of variables using large samples of participants. Unfortunately, these same surveys often suffer from issues of low return rates, a lack of in-depth, respondent-specific questions, and, in many cases, the inability to determine the causal direction of associations. In contrast, small focus groups, while able to produce description-rich data

---

[10] The Burned Furs were a group of furries who opposed public promotion or discussion of furries' sexuality, especially within the context of the fandom, which, they argued, was the cause of the furry fandom's poor public perception. Critics of the movement contended that the Burned Furs represented an anti-sexuality hate group. The Burned Furs movement was active from 1998 until 2001, though many of the movement's beliefs continue to be debated among furs to this day.

that accurately portray the experience of individual furries, suffer from the problem of being too small and idiosyncratic to represent the entire furry fandom.

Because any one study will have flaws, the IARP has collected data using numerous different methodologies, including international internet surveys, convention-based surveys, experiments conducted at conventions, focus groups, individual interviews, and computer-based reaction time experiments. Using diverse methods allows researchers to find converging evidence for a hypothesis, triangulating on answers with multiple sources of data. This principle has been at the core of the IARP's research, and much of the evidence has been collected and replicated across multiple types of studies and across several samples of furries (e.g., internet samples, convention-based samples).

To Whom Are Furries Being Compared?

Researchers endeavor to find appropriate control groups to compare their group of interest against. Knowing how furries score on a 7-point scale of religiosity or political liberalism is more meaningful when there are other groups with whom to compare the numbers. Across more than five years of research, the IARP has sought numerous control groups (e.g., sport fans, community members, anime fans) against which to meaningfully compare furries.

In many instances, furries are simply compared to non-furries. In early studies, non-furry samples consisted of attendees at furry conventions who did not call themselves furries—this included hotel and security staff, vendors, and parents and friends of furry attendees. This comparison group was chosen, in part, because of the IARP's limited resources and the group's availability. There are obvious limitations to these early control groups, including the fact that non-furry convention-goers may have more positive attitudes toward furries than, say, the average American. In response to this limitation (and gaining funding), later surveys sought better control groups, including undergraduate psychology students and representative American samples recruited through websites such as Amazon's Mechanical Turk.

More recently, the IARP has sought out more meaningful control groups. In a recent set of studies, participants included members of other fan groups as well. In some studies, participants were fans of anything (e.g., music, *Doctor Who*). In other studies, participants were recruited based on their identity as a member of specific fan groups—anime fans (self-described fans of Japanese-style animation and graphic novels) represent a fandom with significant content overlap with the furry fandom, while fantasy sport fans (people who create fantasy sport teams and compete against others in recreational leagues using real-world sporting event data) represent a fandom with little content overlap. Prior research verified that furries considered anime fans to be similar to furries, and fantasy sport fans to be quite dissimilar from furries (Plante, Roberts, Snider, Schroy, Reysen, & Gerbasi, in press).

What Is A Furry?

To this point, we have defined the groups that furries are being compared to, but we have not yet defined furries. The IARP defines furries as self-identified fans of anthropomorphism—the ascription of human traits to animals—or zoomorphism—the ascription of animal traits to humans. This definition has several important implications. First, it makes no assumptions about any one attitude, belief, or action being, in and of itself, definitively furry. Put another way: no one behavior or belief objectively and certainly makes a person a furry. For example, one could wear a fursuit, but nevertheless not call themselves a furry (they may be a sporting team mascot). Secondly, our definition suggests that furry is a self-imposed label, comparable to other labels people use to identify themselves (e.g., liberal, running enthusiast). As such, while others may apply the "furry" label to someone, our definition emphasizes the psychological effects of internalizing and integrating "furry" into one's own identity—of applying the label to oneself.

To summarize, furries are people who apply the label of "furry" to themselves, regardless of how their interest in anthropomorphism or zoomorphism manifests itself (e.g., fursuiting, spiritual beliefs, interest in producing/viewing artwork, fursona creation, etc.) The rest of this chapter summarizes some of the basic findings of half a decade of furry research, starting with demographic variables. We then review data about fandom-specific content. Finally, we review how furries score on various psychological scales relative to other groups.

Furry Demographics

Before delving into the furry psyche, we should first know some basic information about the furry fandom's composition. Demographic information can guide our interpretation and understanding of the fandom's content and our interpretation of furries' responses on psychological measures.

We begin by investigating whether our furry samples overlap with our comparison samples. For example, if all furries were anime fans and all anime fans were furries, the two groups would be one and the same, making comparisons between the groups meaningless. Knowing the extent to which furries overlap with comparison groups allow us to investigate the permeability of the furry fandom compared to other fandoms, a factor which will be discussed in greater depth in the chapter on social identity perspective (see the following chapter).

Research suggests that furries belong to a multitude of fandoms: one in five furries considers themselves to be a brony (an adult fan of the television show *My Little Pony: Friendship is Magic*), while about half of furries consider themselves to be anime fans. By comparison, only about one in ten furries considers themselves to be sport fans (Plante, Roberts, Reysen, & Gerbasi, 2014). These data suggest that there is considerable overlap between the furry fandom and other "nerdy" interests, such as the anime fandom, while, in contrast, there may be far less overlap between furries and more "mainstream" groups, such as sport fans.

Furries are young, but comparable in age to members of similar fandoms. It should be noted that ethics boards have strict research guidelines surrounding minors and thus they are excluded from the studies described. With this caveat in mind, the average *adult* furry is approximately 23-26 years of age, with convention-going furries tending to be about a year older (Plante, Roberts, Reysen, & Gerbasi, 2012). These numbers are comparable to anime fans, but are far younger than fantasy sport fans, who tend to be in their early 30s (Plante, Roberts, Reysen, & Gerbasi, 2014). In comparison, only 12% of furries are in their 30s, with the majority of majority of furries being under the age of 25 (Plante, Mock, Reysen, & Gerbasi, 2011).

As a group, furries are young, and they also tend to get into the fandom at a young age, usually in their mid-to-late teens, a couple of years later than anime fans, and many years earlier than fantasy sport fans, who find their interest in their early-to-mid 20s (Plante, Roberts, Reysen, & Gerbasi, 2014; Plante, Roberts, Reysen, & Gerbasi, 2012.) Most furries indicate that there was a gap, typically a year or two, between the time they began identifying as a furry and the time they began actively participating in the furry fandom (Plante, Roberts, Reysen, & Gerbasi, 2012).

The furry fandom is about 80% male, a number consistently found across online and convention-going samples (Plante, Roberts, Reysen, & Gerbasi, 2012). This number is comparable to online anime fans, who are also predominantly male, although convention-going anime fans were almost equally male and female (Plante, Roberts, Reysen, & Gerbasi, 2014). The furry fandom also has a significant transgender population: double that of the anime fandom and four times that of the fantasy sport fandom (Plante, Roberts, Reysen, & Gerbasi, 2014). There has been little research investigating the reason for this greater-than-average proportion of transgender individuals in the furry fandom, though there is evidence (discussed later in this chapter) suggesting that the furry fandom is an open and accepting place for members of stigmatized minority groups, making it inviting for transgender individuals and increasing the likelihood that a transgender individual may feel comfortable "coming out" to others as their felt gender.

The furry fandom is predominantly White, with only about one in ten furries identifying as a member of a non-White ethnic group (Plante, Roberts, Reysen, & Gerbasi, 2012, 2014). In contrast, the anime fandom and the fantasy sport fandom have far more Asian and Black members, respectively (Plante, Roberts, Reysen, & Gerbasi, 2014).

Furries, as a group, are particularly liberal-minded, having been shown, across a pair of studies, to score significantly more liberal on a scale of political orientation than the average American (Plante, Roberts, Reysen & Gerbasi, 2012), convention-going anime fans, and fantasy sport fans (Plante, Roberts, Reysen & Gerbasi, 2014). These results are consistent with furries' relatively young age and the prevalence of gay, bisexual, and alternative sexual identities in the furry fandom, the latter of which is discussed below. Moreover, evidence suggests that furries' liberal attitudes are driven predominantly by social liberalism (e.g., progressive attitudes regarding gay marriage), and not by economic liberalism (e.g., welfare programs), about which furries are far more moderate (Plante, Reysen, Roberts, & Gerbasi, 2013).

In accordance with furries' liberal political beliefs, furries are also significantly less religious than other groups: convention-going anime fans, fantasy sport fans, and the average Americans (Plante, Reysen, Roberts, & Gerbasi, 2012, 2014). About half of all furries identify as atheist or agnostic, while the other half identify with various other beliefs, the most popular of which is Christianity (Plante, Reysen, Roberts, & Gerbasi, 2012). Despite the fact that furries, as a group, do not consider themselves to be particularly religious, many do endorse spiritual beliefs, including a reverence for nature outside of conventional religious doctrine (Plante, Reysen, Roberts, & Gerbasi, 2012).

Several indicators of socioeconomic status have been

studied in the furry fandom. As a group, furries are well-educated, with most furries reporting some form of completed or in-progress post-secondary education (including trades, certificates, and degrees), a number comparable to anime fans, but less than that of fantasy sport fans—in part owing to fantasy sport fans' older age (which increases the likelihood of attending and completing post-secondary education; Plante, Mock, Reysen, & Gerbasi, 2011; Plante, Roberts, Reysen, & Gerbasi, 2014). About half of furries currently reside with their parents (Plante, Reysen, Roberts, & Gerbasi, 2013). While, on the surface, this may seem to suggest that furries are unemployed or lacking in self-sufficiency, data suggest that furries' annual income does differ significantly from a control sample of Americans (Plante, Roberts, Reysen, & Gerbasi, 2014). This difference is likely driven by the fact that many furries are young and still in college, and data suggest that, as furries get into their mid-twenties, they tend to move out to live with a spouse or partner or with a friend (Plante, Reysen, Roberts, & Gerbasi, 2013). In this regard, the data suggest that, as a fandom, furries are comparable to other groups of young, college-age students.

The IARP has also examined furries' families and relationships. Furries were no more likely than a non-furry control group to have had parents who were divorced (Plante, Roberts, Mock, Reysen, & Gerbasi, 2011). One study suggested that, for furries with siblings, they were significantly more likely to be the older sibling than the younger sibling (Plante, Roberts, Mock, Reysen, & Gerbasi, 2011). There is little explanation for this difference, and it remains a subject for future research to investigate.

Moving beyond familial relationships, studies suggest that about half of furries report their current relationship status as "single", a number significantly lower than in the anime fandom, but significantly higher than the fantasy sports fandom, where participants, being much older, are far more likely to be married (Plante, Roberts, Reysen, & Gerbasi, 2014). Furries' relationships are far more likely to be in open or polyamorous than anime fans or fantasy sport fans, a finding not yet fully explained, but which may reflect the furries' previously-stated liberal-mindedness (Plante, Roberts, Reysen, & Gerbasi, 2014).

Even more interesting than the composition of their interpersonal relationships, however, is the sexual orientation of furries as compared to other groups. Furries are about six times more likely than the average American to self-identify as predominantly or exclusively homosexual, and were also more likely to self-identify as bisexual or with another sexual orientation (Plante, Roberts, Reysen, & Gerbasi, 2014). Put another way, approximately 25% of the furry fandom self-identifies as homosexual, while only about one in three furries self-identifies as heterosexual. Homosexuality was also far more prevalent in the furry fandom than in the anime fandom, a group with considerable overlap with the furry fandom demographically, suggesting that the prevalence of sexual minorities is a distinct feature of the furry fandom, with one exception: furries were no more likely to be asexual than members of the anime fandom (Plante, Roberts, Reysen, & Gerbasi, 2014).

Taken together, the demographic data allow us to understand the general composition of the furry fandom as being one that, while comparable to other groups of young, educated, middle-class Americans, is also distinct in its predominantly white male composition, its liberal-mindedness, and its large proportion of sexual minority group members. With this context and these idiosyncrasies in mind, we can now interpret trends in furry-specific variables.

Furry Fandom Content

While we have previously defined furries as people who share an interest in anthropomorphism or zoomorphism, this definition fails to capture the numerous idiosyncrasies and nuances of the furry fandom. Unlike media-specific fan groups, where members organize around a shared interest in a specific team, television show, literary genre, or band, furries organize around a far more nebulous, less-defined interest. An interest in anthropomorphism can manifest itself via television shows, movies, comics, stories, and artwork featuring walking, talking cartoon animals. Alternatively, this interest may be the product of deep spiritual connections with non-human animals. Others may show their interest by wearing elaborate, mascot-style fursuits, or simply by admiring and learning about animals with others who share the same passion. Put simply, the furry fandom represents a group of people with a broad assortment of interests who, as the research discussed in this chapter and the chapters that follow show, nevertheless feel a strong sense of community.

One of the few nearly-universal aspects of the furry fandom is the fursona. Nearly all furries have a fursona—an anthropomorphic avatar or representation of themselves (Plante, Roberts, Reysen, & Gerbasi, 2013a). Fursonas usually consist of a name and a species, and can vary immensely in their specificity, including color, sub-species or hybrid species composition, personality traits, character history, significant relationships, and special abilities. Nearly half of furries say they have only ever had one fursona to represent themselves, and very few furries indicated having more than three or four fursonas throughout their life (Plante, Roberts, Reysen, & Gerbasi, 2013a). Among those furries who have had multiple fursonas, they usually report identifying with one fursona at a time (Plante, Roberts, Reysen, & Gerbasi, 2013a). In other words, most furries identify with a single fursona, though that fursona may change over time as another species or character comes to better represent who they are.

Fursonas represent the "face" that furries present to other members of the fandom. Given the predominantly online nature of the fandom (discussed later in this section), many furries interact with one another through their fursonas, either in online forums, chat sessions, or social websites. As such, furries spend a lot of time thinking about their fursonas. For most furries, the process of fursona creation is something personally significant and meaningful, as they imbue their fursonas with characteristics and personalities that reflect their own traits (Plante, Roberts, Reysen, & Gerbasi, 2013a). When furries do create fursonas that differ from themselves, they tend to create fursonas that represent more idealized versions of themselves (Plante, Roberts, Reysen, & Gerbasi, 2013a). These idealized selves are more attractive, confident, friendly, and playful versions of themselves, who are also less shy, intolerant, and introverted (Plante, Roberts, Reysen, & Gerbasi, 2013a). In sum, the process of fursona creation or discovery is, for many furries, a meaningful and deeply personal process.

When it comes to fursona species, trends and popular species exist in the fandom. For example, the most frequently identified fursona species are wolves, foxes, dogs, large felines (e.g., tigers, lions), rabbits, otters, reptiles, bears, horses, and dragons, this last species illustrating that furries are neither bound by the constraints of reality, nor are they restricted to furred species (Plante, Mock, Reysen, & Gerbasi, 2011). Many of these species are domesticated animals (e.g., dogs and cats), or are species which have been popularized in media portrayals (e.g., *The Lion King*) or which have cultural significance (e.g., wolves and Indigenous American spiritual beliefs). A small minority of furries has a fursona based on a hybrid of more than one species, while another minority has a fursona based on a mythical or non-existent species (Plante, Mock, Reysen, & Gerbasi, 2011).

Our research suggests there are no personality differences between furries who choose one species over another (Plante, Mock, Reysen, & Gerbasi, 2011). Furries recognize this to be the case, as most agree that fursona species does not weigh into the decision of whether or not they interact with a person (Plante, Reysen, Roberts, & Gerbasi, 2012). Despite the fact that most furries do not judge others by their fursona species, however, many furries believe that a person's fursona species is nevertheless informative about that person (Plante, Reysen, Roberts, & Gerbasi, 2012). Given that many furries identify at least somewhat with stereotypes and traits associated with their fursona species, there may be some justification for these beliefs.

Furries do not exist in a social vacuum—a big part of understanding furries involves understanding the ways furries interact with one another. Most furries interact with one another online, using furry forums, message boards, and instant messaging programs as part of their daily routine (Plante, Roberts, Mock, Reysen, & Gerbasi, 2011). The fandom also has a significant real-world presence: most furries say they attend local furry meet-ups at least a few times per year, and about half of all furries say they attend one or more furry conventions every year (Plante, Roberts, Mock, Reysen, & Gerbasi, 2011). It is at these face-to-face gatherings of furries where fursuits—the most visually recognizable aspect of the furry fandom—are found.

Costing hundreds or thousands of dollars and often representing hundreds of hours of artistry, fursuits are, for many, a way to interact with others in the real world—furry and non-furry alike—as their fursona. Despite the common misconception that furries are "people who wear fursuits," only one in four furries owns even a partial fursuit[11] (Plante, Roberts, Mock, Reysen, & Gerbasi, 2011). Fursuits are often prohibitively expensive or difficult to construct for those who would like to own one, and many furries indicate that they have no interest in owning a fursuit. Is it also worth noting that fursuits are just one way furries can "wear" their interest in anthropomorphism. In fact, the most popular accessories include tails, furry-themed clothing, and collars (Plante, Reysen, Roberts, & Gerbasi, 2014). And while many furries display their interest through worn visual expressions, some have no interest in visual displays of their interest—contrary to popular stereotypes and media misconceptions, which often define furries as people who wear fursuits (e.g., McMahon, 2009).

---

[11] Partial fursuits, which usually consist of a head, tail, hands and/or feet, are contrasted with full fursuits, which include the torso and cover nearly the entire body. Only about half of fursuits owned are full, due to prohibitive cost or the wearer's preference to avoid the hassle or discomfort of wearing a full-body suit.

One of the most central aspects of the furry fandom is the creation of furry-themed content: furries frequently identify visual art and writing as central aspects of furry culture, and furry artists, writers, and musicians are held in high regard in the furry community (Plante, Roberts, Mock, Reysen, & Gerbasi, 2011). Many furries cite furry artwork, often discovered through the internet—as one of the most important contributors to their own furry interests, and about one in three furries consider themselves to be artists, significantly more than in comparable fandoms such as the anime fandom (Plante, Roberts, Mock, Reysen, & Gerbasi, 2011; Plante, Roberts, Reysen, & Gerbasi, 2014).

Given the centrality of artwork in the furry fandom, as well as the popular stereotype of the furry fandom as being nothing more than a fetish, it is worth asking about the role of sexuality in the fandom. As one would expect in any fan group comprised of young adults, the vast majority of furries view pornography that combines their naturally-occurring sexual interest with themes from their interest: the vast majority of furries view pornography that contains furry-related themes (e.g., involving anthropomorphized animal characters), although male furries are more likely to do so than female furries (Plante, Reysen, Roberts, & Gerbasi, 2013). Despite the prevalence of furry-themed pornography in the fandom, however, most furries disagree that pornography and sexuality are defining features of, or the central draw to, the furry fandom: most furries show little to no strong preference for pornographic furry art over non-pornographic furry art, and many furries reference the fandom's open and accepting nature and sense of community, not pornography or sexuality, as the defining motivator of their fandom involvement (Plante, Reysen, Roberts, & Gerbasi, 2013; Plante, Mock, Reysen, & Gerbasi, 2011). Compared to anime fans, furries are more likely to own pornographic material, but they are also significantly less likely to own violent material, and they are just as likely to also own non-pornographic material (Plante, Roberts, Reysen, & Gerbasi, 2014). Taken together, the data suggest that while sexual themes are present in the furry fandom, they are neither defining nor necessary features of most furries' interests.

For many furries, the fandom is, first and foremost, a place where they can interact with friends who accept them and share a similar interest (Plante, Roberts, Mock, Reysen, & Gerbasi, 2011). Illustrating this point, most furries agree that in addition to identifying with furry interests, they also strongly identify with others in the fandom who share their interest (Plante, Roberts, Reysen, & Gerbasi, 2013a). In fact, furries are significantly more likely than anime or fantasy sport fans to identify with other members of their fan community (Plante, Roberts, Reysen, & Gerbasi, 2014). Furries say that about half of their friends are also furry, and many furries, especially those who are homosexual, say that they found their current relationship partner in the furry fandom (Plante, Roberts, Reysen, & Gerbasi, 2013a, 2014). Taken together, these data illustrate the significance of the relationships furries forge within the fandom.

In sum, the furry fandom often evades simple definition, given its relatively broad and ill-defined nature. Research has revealed several common elements of the furry experience, most of which are either inaccurately portrayed or completely ignored by popular media, including fursona creation, furry artwork and writing, and the importance of belonging to a community of like-minded others.

Psychological Questions about Furries

In this section, we move beyond idiosyncrasies in the content of the furry fandom and introduce psychological questions about furries. Several of these topics will be discussed in greater detail in later chapters and have been discussed at length in peer-reviewed scientific journal articles. This section is intended to be a general overview of some of the questions being investigated by psychologists about furries and the furry fandom.

One of the first questions the IARP asked about furries involved the boundary between "human" and "non-human":

are furries people who see themselves as animals, or just people who like animals and animal-themed artwork? Research on this question has revealed an important distinction between furries—people with an interest in anthropomorphism—and *therians*[12]—people who self-identity with non-human animals. Across numerous samples, data have consistently shown that, contrary to stereotypes which suggest that furries are people who identify as non-human animals, only about 17% of furries self-identify as therian (Plante, Reysen, Roberts, & Gerbasi, 2013).

While furries are more likely than the average American to say they do not feel entirely human and that they would become non-human if they could, furries are far less likely to agree with these statements than therians (Plante, Reysen, Roberts, & Gerbasi, 2012; Plante, Roberts, Reysen, & Gerbasi, 2012). As such, it seems that furries fall somewhere between non-furries and therians with regard to how they see themselves relative to animals, though it is worth noting that the majority of furries consider themselves to be human and do not wish to change that. It is also important to note that among those who said they did not feel fully human, this belief was not based on physical characteristics: they were five times more likely to say that the nature of their non-human identification was psychological or spiritual, not physical (Plante, Roberts, Reysen, & Gerbasi, 2012). In other words, those who feel not entirely human are far more likely to base this on having the mindset or a felt spiritual connection to a non-human animal than to actually see themselves as having a non-human animal's physical traits.

The IARP has also been interested in escapism and magical

---

[12] It is worth noting that there exists an even finer distinction between therians and otherkin. While definitions of each group are somewhat contested, "therian" generally refers to a person who identifies, in whole or in part, with a non-human animal species. In contrast, "otherkin" generally refers to a person who identifies, in whole or in part, with a non-human, fictional entity (e.g., a dragon).

thinking among members of the furry fandom. Given the prevalence of artists and writers in the furry fandom, and the regularity with which furries encounter impossible hybrids or non-existent animal species as fursonas, we have investigated whether being furry is associated with magical thinking. Indeed, evidence suggests that the more strongly a person identifies as a furry, the more likely they are to possess magical beliefs— unusual or supernatural thoughts and hypersensitive senses – and to experience more vivid mental images and even visual hallucinations (Plante, Roberts, Reysen, & Gerbasi, 2013b).

While in some contexts, these unusual beliefs and sensations might be considered pathological, IARP research on furries shows that furries, while engaging in more fantasy than non-furries, tend to do so in relatively healthy ways, not pathological ones; for example, while furries are more likely to engage in fantasy to escape from undesirable aspects of their day-to-day lives, they are also more likely to use fantasy to motivate themselves or to cope with failure, as a means of self-expression, or as a form of recreation (Plante, Reysen, Roberts, & Gerbasi, 2013; Plante, Roberts, Reysen, & Gerbasi, 2012). In other words, furries may be more likely to entertain magical or supernatural thoughts than non-furries, but this does not predict dysfunction and, if anything, suggests that furries' active fantasy lives, more often than not, are a source of leisure and self-expression.

In a similar vein, given the unconventional nature of furries' interests and their vivid and active fantasies, the IARP has been investigating whether furries are more likely than non-furries to have been diagnosed with a psychological disorder. To date, there has been no evidence to suggest that being a furry is associated with an increased likelihood of having a medical disorder, using psychiatric medication, or having attention-deficit/hyperactivity disorder, an anxiety disorder, or a mood disorder (Plante, Roberts, Reysen, & Gerbasi, 2013b). There is, however, preliminary evidence suggesting that furries may be more likely to be diagnosed with Asperger's Syndrome, a form of high-functioning autism, although it remains the goal of future research to replicate these findings and determine the reason for this relationship (Plante, Roberts, Reysen, & Gerbasi, 2013b). Research on well-being has consistently shown that furries experience psychological well-being comparable to that of non-furries. For example, furries do not differ significantly from a sample of average Americans with regard to self-esteem, felt psychological and physical health, and relationships and, in fact, there is evidence to suggest that furries may have a better-developed, more stable sense of identity than non-furries (Plante, Roberts, Reysen, & Gerbasi, 2012). Other research has shown that, compared to members of other fandoms (e.g., anime, fantasy sports), furries are just as happy with their lives and feel just as good about themselves as similarly-aged others (Plante, Roberts, Reysen, & Gerbasi, 2014).

To summarize, the IARP is beginning to understand many important psychological processes operating within the furry fandom. Research on furries is helping to answer questions about the nature of the boundary between humans and non-human animals, questions about the nature and effects of active fantasy life, and the problems associated with being a member of a stigmatized minority group and the possible benefits that being a member of an open and accepting community can provide.

Conclusion

Throughout this chapter, we have reviewed what the IARP has begun to learn about the furry fandom. Through the use of converging methodology that compares furries to interesting control groups, researchers have shed light on a group which, for years, has been known to most only through stereotypes and misconceptions. Demographic information provides a first look at the fandom and the social context through which to interpret other findings. A look at the idiosyncrasies and trends in the fandom helps us to better understand the experience of the average furry and what the fandom is and is not. Finally, a look at some of the psychological mechanisms associated with the furry fandom illustrates that, far from being trivial or insignificant, time spent in the furry fandom can have real, lasting effects on furries.

References

Burned Furs. (n.d.). Retrieved December 15, 2014 from Wikifur: http://en.wikifur.com/wiki/Burned_Furs

Gurley, G. Pleasures of the fur. *Vanity Fair* (2001). March, 174-196. (Accessed online at: http://www.vanityfair.com/culture/features/2001/03/furries200103?currentPage=1)

McMahon, T. (Writer, Director), Arnarson, H. A. (Writer), Miller, G. (Writer). (2009). Death Over Easy: Em-Bear-Assed [Television series episode]. In Original Productions (Producer), *1000 Ways to Die*. New York, NY: Spike.

Mock, S. E., Plante, C. N., Reysen, S., & Gerbasi, K. C. (2013). Deeper leisure involvement as a coping resource in a stigmatized leisure context. *Leisure/Loisir, 37,* 111-126.

Plante, C. N. (2014, April 22). Trade-Offs in Furry Research: [adjective][species] vs. The IARP. Article retrieved from http://adjectivespecies.com/2014/04/22/trade-offs-in-furry-research-adjectivespecies-vs-the-iarp/

Plante, C. N., Mock, S., Reysen, S., & Gerbasi, K. C. (2011). *International Anthropomorphic Research Project: Winter 2011 Online Survey Summary*. Retrieved from https://sites.google.com/site/anthropomorphicresearch/past-results/international-online-furry-survey-2011

Plante, C. N., Reysen, S., Roberts, S. E., & Gerbasi, K. C. (2012). *International Anthropomorphic Research Project: Furry Fiesta 2012*. Retrieved from https://sites.google.com/site/anthropomorphicresearch/past-results/furry-fiesta-2012

Plante, C. N., Reysen, S., Roberts, S. E., & Gerbasi, K. C. (2013). *International Anthropomorphic Research Project: Furry Fiesta 2013 Summary*. Retrieved from https://sites.google.com/site/anthropomorphicresearch/p

ast-results/furry-fiesta-2013

Plante, C. N., Reysen, S., Roberts, S. E., & Gerbasi, K. C. (2014). *International Anthropomorphic Research Project: Furry Fiesta 2014 & Longitudinal Study Wave 2 Summaries*. Retrieved from https://sites.google.com/site/anthropomorphicresearch/past-results/2014-furry-fiest

Plante, C. N., Roberts, S. E., Mock, S., Reysen, S., & Gerbasi, K. C. (2011). *International Anthropomorphic Research Project: Anthrocon and Summer 2011 Survey Summary*. Retrieved from https://sites.google.com/site/anthropomorphicresearch/past-results/international-furry-survey-summer-2011

Plante, C. N., Roberts, S. E., Reysen, S., & Gerbasi, K. C. (2012). *International Anthropomorphic Research Project: Anthrocon 2012 and 2-Year Summary*. Retrieved from https://sites.google.com/site/anthropomorphicresearch/past-results/anthrocon-2012-iarp-2-year-summary

Plante, C. N., Roberts, S. E., Reysen, S., & Gerbasi, K. C. (2013a). *International Anthropomorphic Research Project: 2013 Fursona Survey Summary*. Retrieved from https://sites.google.com/site/anthropomorphicresearch/past-results/2013-fursona-survey

Plante, C. N., Roberts, S. E., Reysen, S., & Gerbasi, K. C. (2013b). *International Anthropomorphic Research Project: Anthrocon 2013 Summary*. Retrieved from https://sites.google.com/site/anthropomorphicresearch/past-results/anthrocon-2013

Plante, C. N., Roberts, S. E., Reysen, S., & Gerbasi, K. C. (2014). *International Anthropomorphic Research Project: 3-Fandom Project (Furries, Anime Fans, & Fantasy Sport Fans)*. Retrieved from https://sites.google.com/site/anthropomorphicresearch/past-results/iarp-2014---3-fandom-project

Plante, C. N., Roberts, S. E., Snider, J. S., Schroy, C., Reysen, S., & Gerbasi, K. C. (in press). 'More than skin-deep': Biological essentialism in response to a distinctiveness threat in a stigmatized fan community. *British Journal of Social*

Psychology.

Roberts, S. E., Plante, C. N., Gerbasi, K. C., & Reysen, S. (in press). Clinical interaction with anthropomorphic phenomenon: Notes for health professionals about interacting with clients who possess this unusual identity. *Health & Social Work.*

Shermer, M. (2002). *Why People Believe Weird things: Revised and Expanded.* New York, NY: Henry Holt and Company.

Zuiker, A. E. (Writer), Stahl, J. (Writer), & Lewis, R. (Director). (2003). Fur and Loathing [Television series episode]. In J. Bruckheimer (Producer), *CSI: Crime Scene Investigation.* Los Angeles, CA: CBS Paramount Network Television.

SOCIAL IDENTITY PERSPECTIVE OF THE FURRY FANDOM
Doc – Stephen Reysen, Ph.D.

Dr. Stephen Reysen is an Assistant Professor of Psychology at Texas A&M University-Commerce. He teaches classes related to social psychology, intergroup relations, and multicultural diversity. His research interests include topics related to personal (e.g., fanship, threats to personal identity) and social identity (e.g., fandom, global citizenship). His research within the furry community explores issues associated with self and identity.

Stephen Reysen 1
Courtney N. Plante 2
Sharon E. Roberts 2
Kathleen C. Gerbasi 3

1 Texas A&M University-Commerce
2 Renison University College, University of Waterloo
3 Niagara County Community College

Author Note

This research was supported by the Social Sciences and Humanities Research Council of Canada. Address correspondence to Stephen Reysen, Department of Psychology, Texas A&M University-Commerce, Commerce, TX, 75429. E-mail: **Stephen.Reysen@tamuc.edu**

We all associate with a variety of different groups (Reysen, Hall, & Puryear, 2014). For example, a person can view him or herself as a member of a group of people who live in a particular state (e.g., Texans) or nation (e.g., Americans), as part of a group of people with the same sex identity (e.g., male), or as a member of the human species (Reysen, Katzarska-Miller, Nesbit, & Pierce, 2013). Of particular relevance for this chapter, people can also associate themselves with fan groups (Reysen & Lloyd, 2012). Fans are people who are enthusiastic, ardent, and loyal admirers of people, media, or activities. Psychologists distinguish between two different connections experienced by fans: a connection felt with the content itself—fanship—and a connection felt toward others sharing the same interest—fandom (Reysen & Branscombe, 2010). Using the example of a sport fan, that person's fanship represents his or her connection to the Dallas Cowboys, while fandom represents his or her connection to all Dallas Cowboy fans. In other words, fanship is a personal connection with the fan interest, while fandom is the felt connection with the fan group.

While at first glance, it may seem like fandom and fanship are almost the same thing, and research suggests that they are related to one another, they have also been shown to be distinct from one another, as psychologists have shown that fanship is related to some psychological aspects of being a fan that fandom is not, and vice-versa (see Reysen & Branscombe, 2010).

Much psychological research has examined fanship with sport teams (see Wann, Melnick, Russell, & Pease, 2001). Research has also examined sport team fandom. For example, psychologists have examined sport fandom and specific fan behaviors such as game attendance, purchasing team merchandise, and consuming team-related media (e.g., Heere et al., 2011). In fact, the majority of psychological research on fandom and fanship has focused on sport fans, though there has been some research examining excessive fanship in the case of celebrity worship (Schimmel, Harrington, & Bielby, 2007). Despite this excessive focus on sports fans, Reysen and Branscombe (2010) have suggested that the psychological mechanisms underlying fanship and fandom are the same regardless of the specific content of the individual fan's interest. Similarly, it has been suggested that regardless of the fan interest, fans see themselves as connected to the larger community of like-minded fans, even if it is unlikely that they do not personally know all other (or even most other) members of the fan group (Anderson, 1983; Sandvoss, 2005). Put simply, regardless of what a person is a fan of, the psychological phenomena of fans and fan groups are the same across all fandoms.

In the present chapter, we discuss some of the implications of this statement by drawing upon a psychological theory called social identity theory (Tajfel & Turner, 1979; Turner, Hogg, Oakes, Reicher, & Wetherell, 1987). Specifically, we will apply this social identity perspective (described in the next section) to the furry fandom (Gerbasi et al., 2008), which will allow us to better understand the behavior and underlying motivation of furries (for an explanation of the furry fandom see the previous chapter).

Social Identity Perspective

The social identity perspective is a combination of social identity theory (Tajfel & Turner, 1979) and self-categorization theory (Turner et al., 1987), two theories which, when combined, allow researchers to explain psychological processes within and between groups (Hogg & Smith, 2007). Social identity theory explains *what happens* when people think of themselves as part of a group, while self-categorization theory explains *when* people see themselves as part of a group. In this section we will briefly review both theories, beginning with social identity theory and then moving onto self-categorization theory. Interested readers will find fuller explanations of the theories and discussions of other theories that build upon them in existing reviews in the psychological literature (e.g., Hogg & Williams, 2000; Reicher, Haslam, Spears, & Reynolds, 2012; Reicher, Spears, & Haslam, 2010).

Social identity theory (Tajfel & Turner, 1979) states that when it comes to similar others, people are able to consider themselves to be members of the same social group (social identity) rather than seeing themselves and similar others as individuals (i.e., personal identity). This tendency to see one's self as a member of a social group can be so strong that one's group becomes part of his or her self-concept (a mental representation of who he or she is). Put another way, the group is you, and you are the group. This can be illustrated through the example of a person attending a university, let's call him Zac. Zac's self-concept includes aspects of his personal identity: Zac wears glasses, he is tall, he studies engineering, and he enjoys football. Zac's self-concept also contains aspects of his social identities: Zac is on the students' union, he plays on a football team, and he identifies with the Scottish community. Some aspects of Zac's personal identity are more important than others—such as the fact that Zac is studying engineering. Similarly, some aspects of Zac's social identity are more important than others—such as the fact that Zac plays on a football team. Finally, it should be noted that different aspects of Zac's self-concept will be relevant in different situations: Zac's social identity as a member of the students' union may be important for Zac and influence his behavior when he is at school, but it may be far less important to Zac while he is away from school during the summer. In other words, the salience of social identities is context-dependent, and some identities are more relevant in some contexts than others.

One central tenet of social identity theory states that the groups that are relevant or on your mind in any given situation affect how you see yourself and others. When you mentally place yourself within a group (e.g., "I am a furry"), you begin to feel a psychological connection to the group—termed ingroup identification. Group members naturally compare the ingroup to relevant outgroups as a way of evaluating the ingroup's status on relevant dimensions. Take, for instance, a furry stating that "furries are more open and accepting of others than anime fans." In this example, a furry is comparing their ingroup (furries) with a comparable outgroup (anime fans) on a dimension (openness) that is relevant to furries. By focusing on this dimension, furries can increase their self-esteem because this is a dimension on which furries do better than anime fans (furries are more open and accepting), and it is a dimension where furries differ from anime fans (anime fans are not perceived to have this dimension). As this example illustrates, the social identity on one's mind can impact not only how they see themselves, but also how they see others, both ingroup and outgroup members.

Social identity theory also states that people seek to gain and maintain social identities that are both positive—groups we feel good about—and distinct—groups that are different from other groups. People seek positively distinct identities because belonging to positive and distinct groups improves people's self-esteem—their overall evaluation of themselves. To illustrate this, imagine that Jane is a fan of the television show *Doctor Who*. If a report came out saying that *Doctor Who* fans were rated as more intelligent than the average American, then

Jane, who is a member of this group, will feel better about herself as a result of her membership in this positively-evaluated group. If the same report said that the findings were not unique for *Doctor Who* fans, however, but instead said that fans of *any* television show were more intelligent than the average American, the benefit of being a *Doctor Who* fan would be lessened for Jane. This is because the findings were not unique to *Doctor Who* fans, but to any fan of a television show, making it harder for Jane to compare herself favorably to relevant outgroups (such as *Star Trek* fans). If, on the other hand, the report said that only *Doctor Who* fans were uniquely more intelligent than the average American, Jane would receive the biggest boost to her self-esteem of all. This is because of the distinctness of the desirable trait to her identity and her identity alone, allowing Jane to favorably compare herself to all other relevant outgroups. Taken together, this example illustrates the main point of social identity theory that people want to belong to positive and distinct groups. It is worth noting, however, that social identity theory includes far more nuances and complexity than what is detailed here. For example, what happens when it is possible to belong to either a positive group or a distinct group, but not both? Researchers suggest that the motivation to belong to a distinct ingroup may be stronger than the desire to belong to positive groups, as shown in a study where group members were willing to highlight negative characteristics of their own group to increase its distinctiveness from an outgroup (Lemaine, 1974).

Social identity theory also proposed the notion of ingroup favoritism, also known as ingroup bias. In general, group members tend to favor the ingroup. For example, fans of a sport team are more likely to help an injured member of the ingroup than they are to help an injured outgroup member—a fan of a rival team (Levine, Prosser, Evans, & Reicher, 2005). Lastly, the theory also proposes various predictors and strategies that group members utilize to manage one's identity (discussed in Identity Management section).

While social identity theory says that people seek positive

and distinct social identities in service of their self-esteem, self-categorization theory (Turner et al., 1987) expands it by focusing on the details of the categorization process—that is, how people categorize themselves and others into groups. People mentally represent groups with sets of prototypical characteristics specific to each group, called *group content*. These characteristics highlight similarities among members of a group and differences between members of different groups. When an ingroup is salient—that is, the concept is consciously or subconsciously activated in a person's mind, group members will depersonalize themselves by applying the stereotypes of their group to themselves. For example, if openness and tolerance are stereotypical characteristics of furries, then when a furry's identity is made salient (for example, at a furry convention, or when they are spoken to as a furry by non-furries), he or she will tend to see themselves as open and tolerant, as a stereotypical furry. At its core, self-categorization theory states that these prototypical characteristics can change depending on the comparison being made. For example, when compared to anime fans as an outgroup, furries will highlight their openness. However, when sport fans are the salient outgroup, furries may instead activate different prototypical characteristics of furries, such as their care and concern for non-human animals. In this way, group members depersonalize by applying prototypical characteristics that represent the group's shared understanding of who they are—characteristics that highlight similarities among ingroup members and widen the perceived gap between the ingroup and outgroups. As a result, according to self-categorization theory, these depersonalization mechanisms underlie most group processes, including why people conform and why they show ingroup bias (favoring one's ingroup over outgroups).

Self-categorization theory also attempts to explain when different social identities within a person will become salient. There are three "levels" of social identities, varying in terms of how inclusive the group is. The least inclusive of these levels is the personal level, where people see themselves as individuals (e.g., me vs. person sitting next to me). At the intermediate level, people consider themselves as members of distinct, yet somewhat inclusive social groups (e.g., furries vs. anime fans). At the most inclusive level, people categorize themselves as human (e.g., humans vs. non-human animals). The majority of research to date has focused on the intermediate level of categorization, often looking at factors that lead people to make more inclusive or less inclusive categorizations and its effects. For example, a furry may think of him or herself in terms of his/her fursona species (e.g., wolves) compared to people who identify with another fursona species (e.g., cats). That same furry may also think in terms of the more inclusive category of "furry," which includes both wolves and cats. Or that furry may think in terms of being a "fan," which includes furries and anime fans. Whether people adopt more inclusive or less inclusive identities in any given situation is based on both the person and the situation. With regard to the person, he/she needs to know about or have experience with an identity in order to categorize him or herself as a member of it—this is called accessibility, or readiness to view oneself as member of that group. With respect to the situation, self-categorization theory states that the presence of ingroup similarities and between-group differences or the tendency for people to behave as expected based on the content of their group memberships should both influence self-categorization into a more or less inclusive identity. For example, when a furry is at a large comic convention, their identity as a furry may become salient, given that being a furry in this context would make their identity relatively unique compared to the other convention attendees. Alternatively, at a furry convention, a furry's fursona species may become increasingly salient because, in that context, being a "furry" is relatively meaningless, given that most attendees are furries. In contrast, a furry's fursona species provides greater distinctiveness and allows the person to make meaningful comparisons between themselves and others at the convention.

In general, social identity theory and self-categorization

theory suggest that when an identity is salient, greater psychological connection felt with the ingroup (i.e., ingroup identification) predicts adherence to prototypes of the group (Hogg & Smith, 2007). Together, these theories and their hypotheses can be used to explain a wide variety of social psychological phenomena within the furry fandom.

Status and Well-Being

In general, belonging to groups is associated with positive mental well-being (Haslam, Jetten, Postmes, & Haslam, 2009). For example, people who feel a psychological connection to a sport team tend to have greater self-esteem, more positive emotions, greater life satisfaction, and report less loneliness, depression, and negative emotion (see Wann, Waddill, Polk, & Weaver, 2011). Belonging to a group is not always associated with greater well-being, however: the group's status and position within society play an important role in determining whether belonging to the group is beneficial or harmful. For example, as a group, sport fans are relatively high status (compared to a minority fan group such as furries), in part because their interests are mainstream and well accepted by society. As such, a sport fan is unlikely to experience or perceive discrimination from others on the basis of their fan group membership (see Reysen et al., in press). In contrast, those who belong to low status or stigmatized groups perceive discrimination from society which is associated with reduced well-being, especially when the group identity is something a person could conceal (Schmitt, Branscombe, Postmes, & Garcia, 2014).

Despite the potentially detrimental effects of belonging to a stigmatized or low-status group, research has found that there can still be benefits to belonging in such groups. In some circumstances (e.g., for people with multiple piercings), feeling greater psychological connection with a stigmatized group can buffer group members against perceived discrimination and predict positive well-being (e.g., Jetten, Branscombe, Schmitt, & Spears, 2001). One can imagine, for example, that people with multiple piercings and experiencing stigma from society may draw into a close-knit community, the sort that provides social support for its members. Other research has shown that among those with concealable stigmatized identities (e.g., members of sexual minorities), being able to disclose their identity and live authentically with acceptance from a community of like-minded others is also related to greater well-being, particularly when compared to those who have the same identity but choose to conceal it from others (see Chaudoir & Fisher, 2010).

The research on stigmatized group members has recently been applied to the furry fandom. Furries are a group with a concealable stigma: concealable, because a furry can choose not to disclose their furry identity to those around them, and stigmatized because of existing misconceptions and negative stereotypes about furries that are perpetuated by mass media which leads many furries to expect negative responses should their furry identities be discovered (Roberts, Plante, Gerbasi, & Reysen, in press). To test whether being a member of the furry fandom was associated with well-being, as predicted by the reviewed research, Mock, Plante, Reysen, and Gerbasi (2013) asked furries ($N = 3473$) to rate (a) how involved they were in the fandom, (b) their acceptance of their furry identity, (c) the extent to which they disclosed their furry identity to others, and (d) their self-esteem and life satisfaction. The researchers found that the more involved participants were in the furry fandom, then the better their well-being. Furthermore, furries who were more involved in the fandom were more likely to accept their identity as a furry. This acceptance predicted greater disclosure of their furry identity to others (e.g., friends, family), which, consistent with past research, predicted greater well-being (see Figure 1 for a depiction of the model). The results show that actively participating in the furry fandom, despite its stigmatized nature, is related to psychological well-being, in part because this participation in the fandom makes furries feel more accepting of their identity and feel less stress about others discovering their furry identity.

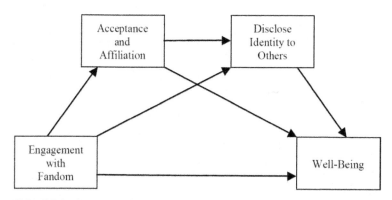

FIGURE 2. Serial mediation model showing mediation of association between engagement with the fandom and well-being through acceptance of identity and disclosure to others (Mock et al., 2013).

Identity Management

According to the social identity perspective, members of a group compare their group to relevant outgroups as a strategy to manage and maintain a positively distinct identity. Tajfel and Turner (1979) specified three key components of this intergroup comparison: *stability, legitimacy,* and *permeability.* The first component, stability, describes whether the status differences between the ingroup and outgroup are perceived to be permanent or temporary. For example, if *Star Wars* fans see themselves as more stigmatized than *Star Trek* fans, then they may think this difference is temporary—caused by the commercial success of the recent *Star Trek* movies—or they may think the difference is permanent—that *Star Wars* fans have, and will always be, more discriminated against than *Star Trek* fans. The second component of intergroup comparisons, legitimacy, describes whether status differences between groups are seen as fair or justified. Continuing with our example, *Star Wars* fans may think the two series are equally good and that there is therefore no good reason for *Star Trek* fans to be less discriminated against than they are. Alternatively, *Star Wars* fans may think, based on the negative reception of the *Star Wars* prequels, that there is a justifiable reason for *Star Wars* fans to be discriminated against. The third component of intergroup comparisons, permeability, describes whether members of one group believe they can join another group (Reysen, Puryear, Katzarska-Miller, Kamble, & Vithoji, 2014). *Star Wars* fans may see the difference between themselves and *Star Trek* fans as impermeable, meaning there is no way for a *Star Wars* fan to become a *Star Trek* fan. Alternatively, *Star Wars* fans may believe that there is nothing stopping them from becoming *Star Trek* fans. Together, the three components of intergroup comparisons—stability, legitimacy, and permeability—are hypothesized by researchers to affect group members' behavior.

According to social identity theory, members of high-status groups strive to maintain this positive and distinct position within the societal hierarchy (Tajfel & Turner, 1979). If a group's status is low, and the boundaries are permeable (it is possible to leave the group), members will leave the low status group for a higher status group (Bettencourt, Dorr, Charlton, & Hume, 2001). When intergroup boundaries are impermeable, on the other hand (it is not possible to leave the low-status group), group members must adopt a different strategy to maintain their positive identity. If the intergroup status difference is seen as stable and legitimate (the difference in status is unlikely to change, and it exists for a valid reason), low-status group members, trapped in these groups, adopt creative strategies to maintain their positive group identity, such as changing the group they are comparing themselves to or changing the dimension they are comparing the two groups on. In a situation where intergroup boundaries are impermeable, intergroup status differences are unstable (i.e., the low-status group may someday become the high-status group), and status differences are seen as unfair, members of low-status groups adopt yet another strategy: they directly challenge the high-status group through collective action and protest behavior. For example, black Americans were a low status group in America. The boundary was impermeable (i.e., black individuals could not leave and join a different ethnic group). Individuals (e.g., Dr. Martin Luther King Jr.) highlighted the notion that black Americans may be equal status in the future (raising a cognitive alternative that highlighted the possible unstable status difference between groups) and noted that the current status difference was illegitimate. In this context (low permeability, low stability, low legitimacy), the lower status group chose to directly challenge the high status group. Groups with a concealable identity—such as furries—have an additional identity management strategy available to them—conceal their identity as a member of the low-status group.

Psychologists have tested whether these components of intergroup comparisons actually affect identity management strategies—particularly identity concealment strategies—in furries (Plante, Roberts, Reysen, & Gerbasi, 2014a). The researchers found that feeling psychologically connected to other furries predicted less concealment of one's identity and greater self-esteem, and, in a pattern similar to Mock and colleagues (2013), disclosing one's furry identity (as opposed to concealing it) was associated with greater psychological well-being. Not all furries disclosed their furry identity, however. Furries who believed that the boundary between "furry" and "non-furry" was permeable were more likely to endorse concealing their furry identity—that is, trying to "pass" as a non-furry (Goffman, 1963, offers an excellent description of this concept). This result can be explained by other research showing that people experience worse well-being in response to discrimination when the stigmatized group is seen as controllable (Schmitt et al., 2014). In other words, when furries believed that being furry was a choice, they were more likely to deny being a furry in response to discrimination, a strategy which, in the long run, predicts reduced well-being.

Threat to the Group

Groups can be threatened in numerous ways, ranging from threatening a group's symbolic or actual existence (Wohl, Branscombe, & Reysen, 2010), to threatening a group's distinctiveness (recall that people seek distinct, positive identities, Branscombe, Ellemers, Spears, & Doosje, 1999). While threatening the very existence of one's group is an obvious threat, distinctiveness threats are less intuitive, and require some explanation. When one's ingroup becomes too similar to an outgroup (e.g., suggesting that Canadians are identical to Americans), ingroup members respond by increasing the distinctiveness of their ingroup (e.g., Americans pointing out ways that they are distinct from Canadians). In another example, Reysen, Snider, and Branscombe (2012) asked fans of the University of Kansas men's basketball team to imagine that their historically named fieldhouse (Allen Fieldhouse) was going to be renamed. Highly-identified fans thought the name change would harm the distinctiveness of the basketball team, which was associated with anger among the highly-identified fans. This sort of anger, seen in the laboratory, is the same anger that fuels protests and reactionary movements to protect ingroup distinctiveness in the real world.

While reactionary movements are one way to deal with distinctiveness threats, there are other strategies. Plante and colleagues (in press) examined whether furries would respond to a threat against the distinctiveness of the furry fandom not by reacting against other fandoms but, instead, changing their beliefs about the furry fandom itself. In particular, Plante and colleagues were interested in beliefs about the essentialism of being furry. *Essentialism* is the belief that members of a group all share an unchangeable group essence that makes them different from other groups (Desmoulin, Leyens, & Yzerbyt, 2006; Yzerbyt, Judd, & Corneille, 2004). After completing a measure of fandom (i.e., identification with the furry community), some of the furries had the distinctiveness of their furry identity threatened by being asked to compare furries to a similar outgroup—anime fans. Other furries, in contrast, were asked to compare furries to a dissimilar outgroup—sport fans, which was not expected to threaten the distinctiveness of furries' identity. A third group of furries was asked to make no comparison at all. Participants then rated the degree to which they believed that being a furry was biologically based (i.e., essentialism). In addition to testing whether furries responded to distinctiveness threats against their furry identity with essentialist beliefs, the researchers also assessed whether furries saw their group as stigmatized, which would make them highly vigilant toward such threats (Major & O'Brien, 2005). In general, most participants did not believe that being a furry was something biologically based. However, highly-identified furries who perceived their group as stigmatized (and were thus vigilant to identity threats) and who were exposed to a distinctiveness threat (comparing furries to anime fans) were more likely to endorse essentialist beliefs about furries—the idea that furries are born as furries. By arguing that furries are biologically born, furries are able to preserve the distinctiveness of their group identity from threateningly similar fan groups, such as anime fans.

Group Content and Prosocial Values

From a social identity perspective, groups have prototypical content—characteristics and norms—that differ from other groups (Turner et al., 1987), and it is this prototypical content that shapes group members' beliefs and behaviors (Hogg & Smith, 2007). Like other groups, the furry fandom has its own prototypical characteristics, one of which is the association of furries with prosocial norms—attitudes and behaviors that are socially helpful and positive. Several illustrations of this prosocial content include furries routinely raising thousands of dollars for animal and environmental charities, the openness and diversity valued by the furry fandom, an expressed desire to help others—furry and non-furry—who are in need, and a general tendency to care about social justice issues (see Plante, Roberts, Reysen, & Gerbasi, 2014b). The prototypical content of the furry fandom is similar to the prototypical content of another group—global citizens. Global citizens are people who endorse attitudes and behaviors related to intergroup empathy and helping, diversity, concern for social justice, support for environmental sustainability, and who generally feel responsibility to improve the world (Reysen, Larey, &

Katzarska-Miller, 2012).

Given the overlap in the prototypical normative group content of furries and global citizens, Plante and colleagues (2014b) examined whether furries would be more likely to endorse values related to global citizenship than a group of non-furries drawn from a random sample of Americans. Furries and non-furries both completed measures related to identifying as a global citizen (Reysen & Katzarska-Miller, 2013). Compared to non-furries, furries were more likely to believe that valued others (friends, family) around them prescribed global citizenship and global awareness. To the extent that furries felt a sense of global awareness and felt like they were surrounded by people who endorsed these norms, they were more likely to view themselves as global citizens. And, to the extent that furries identified themselves as global citizens, they were more likely to endorse six different types of prosocial values, all of which were associated with the prototypical content of global citizen identity (see Figure 2 for a depiction of this model). These results show that engaging with the furry fandom is related to a variety of prosocial values (e.g., environmental sustainability) and awareness of the world. Furthermore, this illustrates that identifying as a furry has implications not just for one's furry identity, but also affects one's tendency to adopt related social identities.

Motivation to Participate in the Furry Community

Social identity researchers have also explored the various motivations that people have to be members of groups. The research tends to show that people have different motivations to belong to groups (see Reysen, Plante, Roberts, & Gerbasi, 2015). Schroy, Reysen, Plante, Roberts, and Gerbasi (2014) examined what motivated furries to participate in the furry fandom. Furries completed psychological measures assessing how strongly furries identified with the furry fandom, as well as a measure of eight different motivations that were found, in previous research, to be the motivating factors to be a sport fan (Wann, 1995). The eight motivations include: (a) eustress

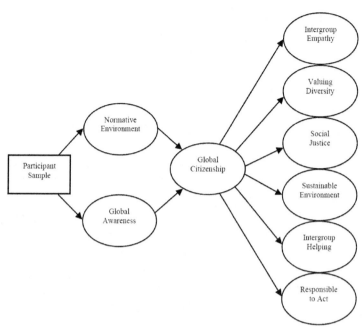

FIGURE 2. Furry fans (vs. community sample) predicting
antecedents, identification, and outcomes of global citizenship
(Plante et al., 2014b).

(positive, functional stress), (b) self-esteem, (c) escapism (avoiding reality), (d) entertainment, (e) economics (earning money), (f) aesthetics (appreciation of beauty), (g) group affiliation (feelings of belonging to a group), and (h) family. The researchers examined which motivations were uniquely associated with the furry fandom. The results showed that furries were motivated to participate in the furry fandom for reasons of belonging to a larger community of like-minded others, entertainment, and family reasons. Furthermore, the motivations for furries differed from other fan groups. For example, fantasy sport fans were motivated by family and aesthetical appeal of sport. Thus, furries are largely motivated to be part of the furry community because the fandom affords furries a sense of belonging.

Future Directions

Much research has been conducted in the past five years looking at the social psychology of the furry fandom. The principles underlying social identity theory and self-categorization theory, which have been found to predict attitudes and behavior in mainstream fan groups, have also been found to apply in a group as idiosyncratic as the furry fandom. While the content of these fandoms may differ wildly, the underlying psychological processes have been shown to be comparable. Despite this research into the antecedents and outcomes of furry fandom participation, however, there remain many more unanswered questions for researchers to explore. For example, given the relatively young age of furries (see the previous chapter), it would be worthwhile for researchers to examine the nature of the interaction between newcomers to the furry fandom and older members of the fandom. Although some research exists examining new fans' interactions with older fans with respect to language usage (Dino, Reysen, & Branscombe, 2009; Reysen, Lloyd, Katzarska-Miller, Lemker, & Foss, 2010), there exists relatively little research examining how new group members come to adopt the attitudes and norms of the fandom they are entering, and the role that older members of the community play in that process (Ashforth, Harrison, & Coreley, 2008). Going forward, it may prove fruitful for researchers to examine how furries learn the norms of their group and how the community maintains the attitudes, beliefs, and norms that are associated with the furry fandom.

A second possible area of future exploration is the stability (or lack thereof) of furries' personalities. Personality psychologists typically argue that personality reflects characteristics or traits that are stable in a person over time (e.g., Funder, 1997). In contrast, social identity theorists argue that personality changes depending on the identity that is salient in any given situation (Reynolds et al., 2010). For example, a psychology professor may appear quite outgoing and friendly in a classroom setting, when his/her "professor" identity is actively on their mind. However, he or she may show a completely different set of personality characteristics—shy and reserved—in another context, such as at a party, where a "nerd" identity is active. Jenkins, Reysen, and Katzarska-Miller (2012) have suggested that the personality traits a person has may reflect the prototypical content of the groups they belong to (i.e., group personality). To test this, researchers may ask furries to report their personalities as individual people, and later report their personalities while thinking about their identities as members of the furry community. From a social identity perspective, we would expect that personality traits would differ between the two measures as a result of which identity was salient (the individual person or the furry identity). It may also be possible that the extent to which furries feel connected to their fursona, which may have its own unique personality traits, may also predict differences in personality, depending on whether a furry's "non-fursona/persona" or "fursona" personality is salient.

Another possible direction for future research would assess the psychological needs that predict whether a furry includes their furry identity in their concept of "self." While furries may identify as a furry, furries differ in the extent to which they tie the concept of "furry" to the concept of "me": for some furries, furry is simply a hobby of theirs, while others, colloquially referred to as "lifers," may consider their furry identity to be a central part of who they are. Building upon the social identity perspective, Brewer's (1991) optimal distinctiveness theory says that group members have two needs that are in direct opposition to one another: the need to feel included in a group (assimilation) and the need to feel like a unique individual (differentiation). As one fulfills one need (e.g., becomes increasingly included in a group), they necessarily increase the other need (e.g., losing their sense of uniqueness by becoming a member of a group). As noted in the previous section, feeling like one belongs in a group is associated with fandom identification. In this research, however, researchers did not measure the extent to which furries saw the furry fandom as distinct from other groups. Future research should examine both of these constructs, distinctiveness and belongingness, with respect to how they contribute to fandom identification. The furry fandom is an open and welcoming community that affords members a way to fulfill their psychological need to belong, while also being a unique and distinct group compared to other groups, which may satisfy the need to be distinct and unique. Optimal distinctiveness may thus explain why many furries feel such a strong sense of psychological connection to the furry fandom, to the extent that the furry fandom fulfills both belongingness and distinctiveness needs.

Conclusion

The present chapter has shown the usefulness of the social identity perspective for psychological research on the furry fandom. The research reviewed has shown that: (a) furries' well-being improves as they engage more with the fandom, (b) furries benefit from the ability to disclose their furry identity, (c) permeable group boundaries strongly predicts whether furries conceal their furry identity when threatened, (d) endorsing essentialist beliefs about furry identity is a strategy adopted by some furries to protect themselves from a distinctiveness threat to the group, (e) engagement in the furry fandom is related to prosocial values and behaviors (including identification with global citizens), and (f) belongingness is perhaps one of the strongest motivations for participation in the community. As the furry fandom continues to grow and as researchers begin to appreciate the need for fan research that goes beyond mainstream fandoms such as sport fans, there will be an ever-expanding set of possible research avenues for psychologists to explore. The present review aims to foster this appreciation and spark future researchers' interest to explore the psychological processes underlying this fascinating and frequently misunderstood group.

References

Anderson, B. (1983). *Imagined communities: Reflections on the origin and spread of nationalism.* London: Verso.

Ashforth, B. E., Harrison, S. H., & Corley, K. G. (2008). Identification in organizations: An examination of four fundamental questions. *Journal of Management, 34,* 325-374.

Bettencourt, B. A., Dorr, N., Charlton, K., & Hume, D. L. (2001). Status differences and in-group bias: A meta-analytic examination of the effects of status stability, status legitimacy, and group permeability. *Psychological Bulletin, 127,* 520-542.

Branscombe, N. R., Ellemers, N., Spears, R., & Doosje, B. (1999). The context and content of the social identity threat. In N. Ellemers, R. Spears, & B. Doosje (Eds.), *Social identity: Context, commitment, content* (pp. 35-58). Oxford, England: Blackwell.

Brewer, M. B. (1991). The social self: On being the same and different at the same time. *Personality and Social Psychology Bulletin, 17,* 475-482.

Chaudoir, S. R., & Fisher, J. D. (2010). The disclosure processes model: Understanding disclosure decision making and postdisclosure outcomes among people living with a concealable stigmatized identity. *Psychological Bulletin, 136,* 236-256.

Desmoulin, S., Leyens, J. P., & Yzerbyt, V. (2006). Lay theories of essentialism. *Group Processes and Intergroup Relations, 9,* 25-42.

Dino, A., Reysen, S., & Branscombe, N. R. (2009). Online interactions between group members differing in status. *Journal of Language and Social Psychology, 28,* 85-93.

Funder, D. C. (1997). *The personality puzzle.* New York: Norton & Company.

Gerbasi, K. C., Paolone, N., Higner, J., Scaletta, L. L., Bernstein, P. L., Conway, S., & Privitera, A. (2008). Furries from A to Z (Anthropomorphism to Zoomorphism). *Society and Animals, 16,* 197-222.

Goffman, E. (1963). *Stigma: Notes on the management of spoiled identity*. Englewood Cliffs, NJ: Prentice-Hall.

Haslam, S. A., Jetten, J., Postmes, T., & Haslam, C. (2009). Social identity, health and well-being: An emerging agenda for applied psychology. *Applied Psychology: An International Review, 58*, 1-23.

Heere, B., Walker, M., Yoshida, M., Ko, Y. J., Jordan, J. S., & James, J. D. (2011). Brand community development through associated communities: grounding community measurement within social identity theory. *Journal of Marketing Theory and Practice, 19*, 407-422.

Hogg, M. A., & Smith, J. R. (2007). Attitudes in social context: A social identity perspective. *European Review of Social Psychology, 18*, 89-131.

Hogg, M. A., & Williams, K. D. (2000). From I to we: Social identity and the collective self. *Group Dynamics: Theory, Research, and Practice, 4*, 81-97.

Jenkins, S. T., Reysen, S., & Katzarska-Miller, I. (2012). Ingroup identification and personality. *Journal of Interpersonal Relations, Intergroup Relations and Identity, 5*, 9-16.

Jetten, J., Branscombe, N. R., Schmitt, M. T., & Spears, R. (2001). Rebels with a cause: Group identification as a response to perceived discrimination from the mainstream. *Personality and Social Psychology Bulletin, 27*, 1204-1213.

Lemaine, G. (1974). Social differentiation and social originality. *European Journal of Social Psychology, 4*, 17-52.

Levine, M., Prosser, A., Evans, D., & Reicher, S. (2005). Identity and emergency intervention: How social group membership and inclusiveness of group boundaries shape helping behavior. *Personality and Social Psychology Bulletin, 31*, 443-453.

Major, B., & O'Brien, L. T. (2005). The social psychology of stigma. *Annual Review of Psychology, 56*, 393-421.

Mock, S. E., Plante, C. N., Reysen, S., & Gerbasi, K. C. (2013). Deeper leisure involvement as a coping resource in a stigmatized leisure context. *Leisure/Loisir, 37*, 111-126.

Plante, C. N., Roberts, S., Reysen, S., & Gerbasi, K. (2014a). Interaction of socio structural characteristics predicts identity concealment and self-esteem in stigmatized minority group members. *Current Psychology, 33,* 3-19.

Plante, C. N., Roberts, S., Reysen, S., & Gerbasi, K. C. (2014b). "One of us": Engagement with fandoms and global citizenship identification. *Psychology of Popular Media Culture, 3,* 49-64.

Plante, C. N., Roberts, S. E., Snider, J. S., Schroy, C., Reysen, S., & Gerbasi, K. (in press). "More than skin-deep": Biological essentialism in response to a distinctiveness threat in a stigmatized fan community. *British Journal of Social Psychology.*

Reicher, S. D., Haslam, S. A., Spears, R., & Reynolds, K. J. (2012). A social mind: The context of John Turner's work and its influence. *European Review of Social Psychology, 23,* 344-385.

Reicher, S., Spears, R., & Haslam, S. A. (2010). The social identity approach in social psychology. In M. S. Wetherell & C. T. Mohanty (Eds.), *Sage identities handbook* (pp. 45-62). London: Sage.

Reynolds, K. J., Turner, J. C., Branscombe, N. R., Mavor, K. I., Bizumic, B., & Subašić, E. (2010). Interactionism in personality and social psychology: An integrated approach to understanding the mind and behavior. *European Journal of Personality, 24,* 458-482.

Reysen, S., & Branscombe, N. R. (2010). Fanship and fandom: Comparisons between sport fans and non-sport fans. *Journal of Sport Behavior, 33,* 176-193.

Reysen, S., Hall, T., & Puryear, C. (2014). Friends' accuracy and bias in rating group identification. *Current Psychology, 33,* 644-654.

Reysen, S., & Katzarska-Miller, I. (2013). A model of global citizenship: Antecedents and outcomes. *International Journal of Psychology, 48,* 858-870.

Reysen, S., Lloyd, J. D., Katzarska-Miller, I., Lemker, B. M., & Foss, R. (2010). Intragroup status and social presence in online fan groups. *Computers in Human Behavior, 26,* 1314-1317.

Reysen, S., Katzarska-Miller, I., Nesbit, S. M., & Pierce, L. (2013). Further validation of a single-item measure of social identification. *European Journal of Social Psychology, 43,* 463-470.

Reysen, S., Larey, L. W., & Katzarska-Miller, I. (2012). College course curriculum and global citizenship. *International Journal for Development Education and Global Learning, 4,* 27-39.

Reysen, S., & Lloyd, J. D. (2012). Fanship and fandom in cyber space. In Z. Yan (Ed.), *Encyclopedia of cyber behavior* (pp. 292-300). Hershey, PA: IGI Global.

Reysen, S., Plante, C. N., Roberts, S. E., & Gerbasi, K. C. (2015). *Optimal distinctiveness and identification with the furry fandom.* Manuscript in preparation.

Reysen, S., Plante, C. N., Roberts, S. E., Gerbasi, K. C., Mohebpour, I., & Gamboa, A. (in press). Pale and geeky: Prevailing stereotypes of anime fans. *The Phoenix Papers.*

Reysen, S., Puryear, C., Katzarska-Miller, I., Kamble, S. V., & Vithoji, N. (2014). Socio-structural intergroup characteristics and group-based emotions in three countries. *International Journal of Intercultural Relations, 43,* 239-252.

Reysen, S., Snider, J., & Branscombe, N. R. (2012). Corporate renaming of stadiums, team identification, and threat to distinctiveness. *Journal of Sport Management, 26,* 350-357.

Roberts, S. E., Plante, C. N., Gerbasi, K. C., & Reysen, S. (in press). Clinical interaction with anthropomorphic phenomenon: Notes for health professionals about interacting with clients who possess this unusual identity. *Health & Social Work.*

Sandvoss, C. (2005). *Fans: The mirror of consumption.* Cambridge, UK: Polity Press.

Schimmel, K. S., Harrington, C. L., & Bielby, D. D. (2007). Keep your fans to yourself: The disjuncture between sport studies' and pop culture studies' perspectives on fandom. *Sport in Society, 10,* 580-600.

Schmitt, M. T., Branscombe, N. R., Postmes, T., & Garcia, A. (2014). The consequences of perceived discrimination for psychological well-being: A meta-analytic review. *Psychological Bulletin, 140,* 921-948.

Schroy, C., Reysen, R., Plante, C. N., Roberts, S. E., & Gerbasi, K. C. (2014). *Motivations as predictors of fanship and fandom in three fandoms.* Manuscript in preparation.

Tajfel, H., & Turner, J. C. (1979). An integrative theory of intergroup conflict. In W. Austin & S. Worchel (Eds.), *The social psychology of intergroup relations* (pp. 33-47). Monterey, CA: Brooks/Cole.

Turner, J. C., Hogg, M. A., Oakes, P. J., Reicher, S. D., & Wetherell, M. S. (1987). *Rediscovering the social group: A self-categorization theory.* Oxford: Blackwell.

Wann, D. L. (1995). Preliminary validation of the sport fan motivation scale. *Journal of Sport and Social Issues, 19,* 377-396.

Wann, D. L., Melnick, M. J., Russell, G. W., & Pease, D. G. (2001). *Sport fans: The psychology and social impact of spectators.* New York: Roultledge.

Wann, D. L., Waddill, P. J., Polk, J., Weaver, S. (2011). The team identification-social psychological health model: Sport fans gaining connections to others via sport team identification. *Group Dynamics: Theory, Research, and Practice, 15,* 75-89.

Wohl, M. J. A., Branscombe, N. R., & Reysen, S. (2010). Perceiving your group's future to be in jeopardy: Extinction threat induces collective angst and the desire to strengthen the ingroup. *Personality and Social Psychology Bulletin, 36,* 898-910.

Yzerbyt, V. Y., Judd, C. M., & Corneille, O. (2004). *The psychology of group perception: Perceived variability, entitativity, and essentialism.* London: Psychology Press.

MARGINALIZATION OF ANTHROPOMORPHIC IDENTITIES: PUBLIC PERCEPTION, REALITIES, AND "TAILS" OF BEING A FURRY RESEARCHER

Dr. Shazzy – Sharon E. Roberts, Ph.D.

Dr. Sharon Roberts is a Canadian sociologist and identity scholar. She is an Associate Professor at Renison University College at the University of Waterloo, and the author of the Identity Issues Inventory (I3). Sharon collaborates with several international teams and applies her studies of identity to eating disorders, anthropomorphism (furries), & youth. Her interests in the furry fandom include fursona (identity) development, pornography, and bullying. She is a proud member of the International Anthropomorphic Research Project, the recipient of a $75,000 SSHRC Insight Development Grant, and is the founder of the Just Like You* *anti-stigma campaign.*

Sharon E. Roberts, PhD 1
Courtney N. Plante, PhD 1
Stephen Reysen, PhD 2
Kathleen C. Gerbasi, PhD 3

1 Renison University College, University of Waterloo
2 Texas A&M University-Commerce
3 Niagara County Community College

Author Note

This research was supported by the Social Sciences and Humanities Research Council of Canada. Address correspondence to Sharon E. Roberts, Department of Social Development Studies, Renison University College – University of Waterloo, Waterloo, Ontario, CANADA, N2L 3G4. E-mail: **serobert@uwaterloo.ca**

I (Roberts) am a furry researcher, as are the rest of the founding members (Gerbasi, Plante, and Reysen) of the International Anthropomorphic Research Project (IARP). I never started out my career thinking that I would ever be an expert on something like the furry fandom. But, here we are. The members of the IARP are some of the first to conduct research aimed at understanding the furry fandom. In an earlier chapter, you can read about how the IARP started, its evolution, and how a few dedicated researchers called into question the veracity of media claims about a group of people with an interest in anthropomorphism. The purpose of this chapter is to flesh out our professional views on the furry fandom, document furries' ascribed status in culture, review some of our history with the media, and discuss the implications of our research as it relates to the human interest side of the furry story.

I admit the first time that I went to a furry convention, in Texas 2012, I did not know what to expect. I knew only one furry, and he was my graduate student at the time. My dear mother, not understanding any of this new area of inquiry, showed concern, but was comforted by the fact that my husband would "scope" out the "threat level" of furries and report back to her. He had the chance to meet some of our local furries because I invited them (via Plante) to crash my faculty Christmas party in 2011 at Renison University College at the University of Waterloo, in Ontario, Canada. I began working at Renison in 2010 as a tenure track assistant professor but was really disappointed to find out there was no fancy-dress Christmas party. So in 2011, I decided that I would add this to my list of things to do. The faculty party was completely left up to me, so I decided to knock up the fun potential by whirling three disco balls and kicking off the party to Michael Jackson's *Don't Stop 'Til You Get Enough* whilst parading my furry guests (who had been hiding through dinner) onto the dance floor to get the dancing portion of the party started. It was *incredible*. After all, furries are *fun*. In conjunction with the party and spending an evening with (the now) Dr. Plante, my husband reported to my mother that she should be most grateful that I was studying furries and not gangsters. There was absolutely no need for concern at all.

When I arrived at my first furry convention, I heard squeaky toy noises, bells, and lots of cheer, smelled some unidentifiable funky things (fursuits are hot, and putting several hundred of them together in an enclosed space can do that—especially if the hotel is poorly ventilated), and saw many colourful suits, excited people, friends delighted to find each other, strangers talking to each other with kindness, people making sure people on the peripheries were included, slightly concerned parents, and oddly, cheerleaders. Why the Radisson had booked both cheerleading groups and furries at the same time was a bit of a mystery to me. Interestingly, this became an issue a couple of years later for our IARP team when we were approached by a television producer to discuss the "conflict" of furries and cheerleaders as part of a show whose premise was something akin to "when vacations go bad," which I discuss further below. My first convention was spent learning the ropes of the research and the fandom. I met Dr. Reysen's team at that time, and learned how to get (i.e., beg) people to fill in furry surveys. The IARP has established a method of handing out surveys while participants waited in long registration lines. As these lines are quite lengthy—up to hours of waiting—the IARP has found that participants are quite willing to fill in our surveys as they wait. It has been a highly successful method of getting great response rates for our research.

It is only because of our long-established history with the fandom that furries trust us with their information. Our team has been especially good at posting some of the basic findings of our research as soon as we have the data inputted, coded, and analyzed, and Dr. Plante has done a great job of keeping our data website up to date with the results of our work. I find it is most pleasurable to see our work being used as evidence in flame wars on Facebook and the like to put the "haters" in their place. Unfortunately, furries are accustomed to facing ridicule, conjecture, and discrimination from those who can hide behind an anonymous avatar in the Internet world of social media. There is a shocking amount of hate directed toward members of the furry fandom.

Furries: The Media-Bruised Community

In the previous three chapters in this book the reader can gain insight into some of the work completed by the IARP. We have tackled many research questions in our tenure together. We have studied basic demographics, sexuality, personal identity, social identity, transition to adulthood, bullying, gender, furry artists, pornography, disabilities in the fandom, spirituality, vegetarianism, animal rights activism, biological essentialism, fursona development, therianthropy, lycanthropy, otherkin identity, and fursuiting.

We have published many of these findings in peer-reviewed journals, although the path to publication is a story worthy of a cocktail in hand. Actually, this whole area of scientific inquiry is perfect fodder for a cocktail party; most people I encounter are curious to learn about furries. Academically, though, we had some doozy-like responses to our work initially—my very favorite response I will share later in this chapter. In the early years, we started writing papers and sending them in for submission in peer-reviewed journals. On one of these reviews, we received a comment that asked, "How do you know that furries are marginalized?"

I guess it was obvious to us. The culture of hate around the furry fandom was unabashed. In Second Life, there was a furry *death camp* (yes, reminiscent of the Holocaust in its conception) where furries could be *disemboweled*. Any quick search on YouTube that involves furries will include negative comments. In fact, there was a song written and posted on YouTube called "Yiff in Hell" with a description of a furry genocide and the slogan "the only good furfag is a dead furfag." The question of what exactly it is that evokes such hostility from the public against furries is still not understood by us—not scientifically anyway. Basic social identity theory teaches the dynamics of ingroup and outgroups differences, but the reactions to furries in the public realm are extreme and likely exacerbated by the media.

In addition to the popular cultural elements that are negative, the media coverage of furries has not been friendly and has fueled that hatred fire. Almost all the inclusion of furries in media and popular culture incorporates blatant sexual activity (e.g., the episode "One Little Word" in the fourth season of *American Dad* shows the characters Stan and Bullock heading to a furry convention where a fursuiter is humped bya carsuiter). A highly unflattering article about furries in *Vanity Fair* (discussed in Gerbasi et al., 2008 and in "'By the Numbers'") was accessed by millions of people. Then there was the *1000 Ways to Die* coverage of an intoxicated guy who "happens upon" a group of furries having an orgy around a fire in the woods. In the episode, the unwitting person tries to have sex with a real bear—confusing it for a furry—and dies via bear attack. Last, lest we forget the coup de grâce of mass-market media misappropriation—the *CSI* episode "Fur and Loathing" (known as the *infamous CSI episode* in the furry world) is a sore spot for most furries. In that episode, furries argue that the portrayal of "costumes" misrepresented the look of a typical fursuit and the descriptions of "furpiles" and "scritching" in the episode were incendiarily hyped to exclude all possibilities other than sexual, deviantly sexual, acts. Actually, I have witnessed an actual furpile, and it is not the stuff of sexual fantasies as envisaged and portrayed by the Hollywood writers. The real pile may be likened more to the beginning of the 1970s show *Eight is Enough* where, in the introductory credits for the show, the family makes a little pyramid of humans and then collapses—yes, sorry to say, but it is really that family-friendly and somewhat banal: people get squished; friends laugh. That's about as sexy as it gets, *Eight is Enough* style.

It feels like it is impossible, sometimes, to change public perception of the furry fandom, although we keep trying. In December 2014, the risks to furries took on a new level. At a furry convention in Chicago, nineteen furries were sent to the hospital and thousands of people evacuated from the hotel after chlorine gas was released in a stairwell. At the time of writing this, it is not clear if it was an accident or intentional, which could make it a terrorist attack, but the police are currently investigating it as a criminal matter. If it *was* an intentional attack, then it is worth noting that chlorine gas is a banned substance for use in *war*. Some of the media coverage of this event was appalling. For example, Mika Brzezinski, an MSNBC correspondent, literally laughed so hard while reporting the attack that she fled the studio. Personally, I fail to see what is funny about nineteen young people being sent to the hospital. I suspect she would not have laughed at a chemical attack on civilians or military personnel for that matter by a rogue regime employing mustard gas, which is what chlorine-related gas was called in the First World War.

So, despite these media events, potential terrorist attacks, YouTube calls for genocide, and the like, we still established, scientifically, that furries were perceived negatively by comparison groups (fantasy sport fans) and published the research findings in *The Phoenix Papers* (Roberts, Plante, Gerbasi, & Reysen, in press). The results showed that furries and bronies are equally disliked, and disliked significantly more than anime fans, who were also perceived negatively by our sample of fantasy sport fans. So, we documented the dislike of furries using science.

The Challenges of Publishing on the Fandom

Our team is certainly making headway with our funding and publishing now, but in the early days, it was not easy. To set up this story correctly, I need to take you inside the research as I (Roberts) experienced it. My first two conventions in Dallas and Pittsburgh were fascinating and exposed me to the furry fandom, but it was really my third convention held in a remote, outdoor location that I attended where I really understood the fandom for the first time. It was like a light was switched on for me, and I became fully supportive of the fandom, but more ultimately shifted part of my focus to advocacy.

Most of the IARP are psychologists, and they are interested in quantitative, objective, and striving for value neutral approaches to understanding this fandom. As a quantitative researcher, I can certainly appreciate that. However, on a previous project that I managed (of government-funded diabetes intervention evaluations, no less), I was exposed to qualitative research methods and triangulation of information. I was inspired to delve into new territory and conduct focus groups and individual interviews.

So, I packed up a six-person research team and flew from Ontario, Canada, to Oklahoma, USA, to study the furries at an outdoor convention, Oklacon. The setting was perfect for conducting this kind of research. Our team had established a question key with the help of the organizers, whom I had met in Texas earlier that year. They were gracious and had a wonderful sense of humor, and I could not have had a more hospitable and welcoming environment in which to get to the heart of the furry matter.

That week, we conducted half a dozen focus groups and many individual interviews. I was overrun with emotion at the raw truth-telling that took place and the degree of vulnerability that lay exposed in those days. I heard people say things like they did not speak to anyone, ever, outside of the fandom. But in that place, at that time, they could be comfortable being themselves. I heard a dozen times that "the fandom saved my life." It was in one of these focus groups that a young man turned the conversational direction by saying, "I wish there was a pamphlet that I could just give to people to explain what it is that I am." And that was when inspiration struck me. I made a promise to these people at that moment that I would become their voice. It should not be the case that a Doctor of Philosophy makes my voice more credible than others' voices, but people tend to listen. And, because of my academic training, I would have access to publishing in peer-reviewed journals, or so I thought.

I came home to Canada inspired to write. Never had a paper held such defined purpose for me. In essence, the paper was directed at healthcare professionals who may encounter an individual with an anthropomorphic identity in their office or practice. The paper basically stated the following: (1) furries find social support within the fandom; (2) the development of a fursona is an important feature of being a furry, and it has benefits for identity development; (3) furries have the capacity to practice developing their social and communication skills in the fandom, and (4) furries fear ostracism, stigma, and discrimination because of their interests in anthropomorphism. Most central to the article, though, was the final point: (5) if the occasion arose, and a furry needed to seek assistance with a counselor, social worker, or physician, then the most crucial thing that worker could do is offer unconditional positive regard if a furry disclosed that part of his or her humanity in a session. In this article, we basically said that furries may present in clinical or medical practice for any number of reasons but because of the stigma attached to being a furry, many were reluctant to tell others about this aspect of their identity. We wanted to intercept and change the potential negative response to the "furry" part of the person on the part of mental health practitioners.

I think my favorite quote from the whole paper (Roberts, Plante, Gerbasi, & Reysen, in press) is this:

"If I have a condition that needs treatment, then it may or may not have anything to do with me being [a] furry. For a successful treatment, I need to embrace the treatment, be invested in it, and want to get better. In order to do that, I need to have a very close, personal relationship of confidence and trust with that clinician, and a part of that, for me, [will be sharing] this aspect of my humanity. This is a part of my life. If [the furry part of me] is not understood by that person, [if the clinician does not understand] that there are positive aspects [of me being a furry] that they can help me focus on, then I'm not going to be able to continue to dialogue."

This seemed pretty reasonable to me. During that trip, I had really seen for the first time what members of the fandom got from this connection with others, and it was special. Life-saving, even, in some cases. I understood why they experienced "post-con depression" (Roberts et al., in press) when they went home. For some of these people, their most sincere human contact and expression with others came at conventions, and they went home to mundane worlds where they hid, were ignored, and had few outlets for sharing their interests.

Journals can vary in their rates of review and publication from a few weeks to years. Usually the editor of the journal will review the paper, and if he or she thinks it is suitable for potential inclusion in the journal, then the editor will locate professors (2-3 usually) to review a blinded version of the paper. Each reviewer documents his or her assessments of all aspects of the submitted paper, makes recommendations for changes (e.g., re-write, re-analyse, more data, control groups, addition theory, etc.). Each reviewer then makes a recommendation to the editor: accept, revise and resubmit, or reject. If the work is of good quality and appropriate to the scope of the journal, reviewers often come back with revise and resubmit recommendations. Editors then compile the reviewers' comments and recommendations, make a decision, and send the authors the news. If authors are invited to revise and resubmit their papers, then the list of revisions can be substantial. Authors make changes and resubmit the work. The journal editor has the right to send out the paper again for review. And so it goes.

So I (we) wrote, revised, and polished the paper so we could send it out for consideration. In December, we submitted the paper to a clinical journal whose name will be withheld. On December 24th, 2012, I received the following response from the journal editor:

"Dear Dr. Roberts,
Wasting our time is really unprofessional.
[Name of Editor]
[Name of Journal]"

What do you do with that? Well, to be honest, I burst into tears. I was utterly confused, and it would seem that my confusion was not to be addressed, as my requests for clarification were left unanswered. Was it the content? Did he think I was trying to spoof him? Was it a quality issue? This last one had me frightened. Was my work *that* bad? A few days later, I sent a copy of the editor's response to a few people to ask them if this was normal—perhaps I just needed to grow a thicker academic skin. There was a consensus that the content of the email was utterly ironic. A few weeks later, I decided that I had to know if it was a quality issue, and so I sent my graduate advisor, Professor James Côté, a copy of the paper and asked him to be brutally candid with me, "Tell me honestly. Is the article a piece of shit?" It might be useful to give a little context to this: Professor Côté, upon receiving my first draft of my dissertation sent me an encouraging, but brutally honest, email with the subject line, *Slowly up the Learning Curve*. I subsequently revised my dissertation five times over the next nine months before he would let it go to defense. When I passed my PhD defense with no revisions, I had only one person to thank. Anyway, I knew that I could trust Professor Côté to be honest with me. His response made me a little teary with relief, "Not at all. Is this the one that was rejected?"

It did not take me long to gain perspective on the whole

issue. I was being dismissed potentially because of the nature of the topic: this was my work on the furry fandom, and yes, it was new, and yes, it was unconventional. But, it is my *work*. For furries, this is *their lives*. The irony of sending an awareness, anti-stigma paper about a poorly-understood and marginalized group of people to a clinical journal whose editor was utterly dismissive to the submission was astoundingly obtuse, and irritatingly, though perfectly, ironic. I was tempted to quote his response back to him with a revised submission that simply added the addendum: "Asked and answered. Q.E.D."

Anyone who knows me, knows that I am tenacious, and I do not wilt in the presence of opposition—especially if I have given my word as I had done to the furry community earlier that year in Oklahoma. It did not take me long to submit the article to another journal, *Health & Social Work*. I was delighted by their acknowledgement of the need for unconditional positive regard of clinicians toward the disclosure of the furry identity in practice. There were the usual revise and resubmit practices, and the paper was accepted for publication. I presented the paper in a talk at the Society for Research on Identity Formation. Even more importantly, the next year, I went back to that small convention and gave the keynote address that featured the published work. It was highly emotional for the audience and for me alike. I felt like I had won a small battle and had come full circle. We had given something back to the furry community. I had enjoyed the smallest taste of justice for furries. And, I wanted to do more.

IARP in the Media

Our team's participation in media coverage has been a rather hit and miss affair. Our first loyalty is to science, of course. But we are also particularly cognizant that the research relationship that we have cultivated with furries and therians over almost a decade is one that is built on trust. That means that each of us on the IARP have reservations about talking to the media if we feel that what we have to say might be misinterpreted, misquoted, or taken out of context in a way that would embarrass us, and as an extension, the fandom. Over the years, we have found ourselves in the position of declining more media coverage than giving interviews. Furries have been so badly burned by sensationalistic media that they no longer allow un-vetted media into many conventions. As an extension, we, as the IARP, worry that our words will, too, be twisted.

For example, as discussed above, our team was approached to discuss a clash of cultures between a group of cheerleaders and furries attending Texas Furry Fiesta in February of 2012. On the Radisson website, there were complaints lodged by a parent who presumably was unhappy with furries. Our team, after much internal debate, decided that we did not trust the show to represent us fairly; with this kind of premise, could we really expect furries to be given a fair "trial" on the show? So, we declined the offer, as did all of the people associated with the convention. I might add, that the only obnoxious behavior that I observed was *not* from the furries. Further, I also asked the hotel staff questions to see if there were issues on that weekend, and there was nothing of significance that happened. In fact, at the world's largest furry convention—Anthrocon in Pittsburgh—the hotel staff always seems pretty jazzed about the furries coming to town. Alas.

On the occasions that we have granted interviews, well, on average, they may be summed up as a colossal waste of time. When the Dr. Phil show contacted our team last year to discuss the furry fandom, both Dr. Gerbasi and Dr. Plante spent, individually, an immense amount (hours and hours of a weekend) with a producer for the show trying to explain to her relevant concepts of the fandom. There was a general concern between Gerbasi and Plante that this producer would not accurately present our information to the public. Gerbasi was told through the weekend that she would be placed on standby during the filming of the show so that if questions came up, then she could go on the show via satellite. After spending the weekend talking to our team, Gerbasi was contacted and told, "We don't need you. We have too much information already." It was hugely frustrating and discouraging.

Several years before, Plante was approached by National Geographic's television show *Taboo*, which was interested in doing an episode about furries. The producers assured Plante that the episode was aimed at presenting furries as "a bit strange, but not dysfunctional or crazy." Moreover, he was being sought out as a researcher who could inject the show with facts and statistics about furries. When the show aired, however, most of the statistics and information was replaced almost entirely by a handful of scenes where Plante and several local furries had donned their fursuits to illustrate what a typical "furry gathering" might look like (e.g., gathering in a park, appearances in public spaces). While the piece was not scathing or incendiary toward furries, it is largely considered to be a missed opportunity to present furry research to a broader audience in a fun and interesting manner.

While Gerbasi prefers to do live interviews, she loathes the need to respond to ridiculous and bizarre questions. Plante recently experienced this in a recorded interview. He was contacted by several news organizations in the wake of the aforementioned chlorine incident to tap his expertise on the fandom. Just a couple minutes into the interview, however, it became apparent that the interviewers were only interested in snagging juicy sound bites. They asked if he could explain, "why furries are into this fetish?" and "what makes furries so strange?" These questions made clear the nature of the story they had in mind. The interview worsened when, having learned that Plante was, himself, a furry, they abandoned all interest in the furry research and, instead, asked him to put on his fursuit and to comment about his own experience as a furry (a request he flatly refused). When the piece aired that evening, none of Plante's interview made it to air, nor was any research or a single credible statistic about furries referenced—though the show did reference the infamous *CSI* episode. To their credit, two different outlets (*The Huffington Post* and *Vox.com*) later interviewed Plante and put out far more representative pieces that referenced IARP research and portrayed furries in a less sensationalist manner.

Sensationalistic portrayals seem to be the more common story when it comes to furries in the media. The fact of the matter is that "furries are about friendship and community," but that does not make for a sensationalistic story, particularly when the audience is expecting scandal and deviance. The truth, however, is that "friendship" and "community" really arethe simplest explanations of the fandom. It is a group of young-ish people (early 20s), mostly male (84%), the majority gay or bisexual (30% exclusively heterosexual), who create an avatar-like character with usually idealistic representations of whom they wish to be, joined by a common interest in anthropomorphized art. They are usually sensitive, smart, and often well-read individuals with diverse political and other interests with a disproportionate likelihood of having experienced bullying in their lifetimes. These people, some of whom struggle to fit with mainstream and some who do not, some of whom are unemployed or on disability *or* high ranking military officials *or* CEOs of companies, all come together to find a group of people whose group identity is rooted in the notion of acceptance of all. These are people who value human connection to others, love animals, raise money for animal charities, and for the most part, mind their own business. *That* is my expert assessment of the members of the furry fandom.

So Where Do We Go From Here?

Over the last few years our team has received data from over ten thousand furries from all over the world. By virtue of developing a strong set of comparisons, we now have the world's largest data set (over three thousand participants) from anime fans, too. In addition, we have studied fantasy sport fans, allowing us to compare three different fan communities in a project we designed and which was funded by the Canadian government through a Social Science Humanities Research Council competition. These grants are extremely difficult to get—usually a 25% success rate in a good year. But we got the grant and we have learned some important things along the way. We are working on publishing the findings of this data, contributing to the anime research community, and we will seek out more funding to continue our work on the furry fandom.

Despite evidence that they function well psychologically (see the previous two chapters), furries nevertheless perceive and experience significant stigma from the world around them. Our one clinical paper is not going to change this reality substantially. As we have discussed extensively, furries are regularly misrepresented in popular media as sexual deviants, immature, or deserving of mockery. Furries often internalize this stigma, leading them to expect non-furries to treat them poorly. As a result, many furries attempt to conceal their furry identity from their friends, family, and co-workers, something they do far more than members of more accepted or mainstream fandoms, such as anime. As a result, many furries—specifically those who are forced to hide their interests and furry identity—experience significant anxiety over the fear of being "outed" and, as a result, they experience reduced well-being (Mock, Plante, Reysen, & Gerbasi, 2013).

At this point, the IARP are working on finding alternatives to the mainstream media. We have begun the process of collecting and producing our own media footage that tells the story rooted in science, not conjecture, prejudice, or "informed" by screenwriters bent on sexing up a story to play on people's fears and distrust of the unknown or the different. We have several projects on the go that we plan to release as we gain funds. One is *Just Like You** which is an anti-stigma outreach for anthropomorphic communities. These will be original public service announcement commercials designed to help the public become interested in learning more about the furry fandom. The second project is *FurScience*—an original educational show designed to provide an accurate public account of the furry fandom. None currently exists. The raw footage (furries' *Speaker's Corner* interviews), which is partially collected, will be fused with existing data/research to produce a quirky, factually accurate media outreach/education project. In 2014, we applied to the Social Sciences Humanities Research Council for a $31,000 grant to help us with this production.

The project was deemed fundable, but that particular completion did not have enough money available to fund the project. We will re-apply for funding when we become eligible in the coming year.

Despite the seemingly negative story for furries, however, there is a silver lining: research suggests that belongingness, acceptance, and a sense of community—many furries identify these as central aspects of being a furry—likely counteract many of the harmful effects of bullying and stigmatization. By belonging to a group of like-minded people, furries are able to be themselves and gain the confidence and sense of community necessary to develop a positive sense of identity (Mock, Plante, Reysen, & Gerbasi, 2013; Roberts, Plante, Gerbasi, & Reysen, in press). It is this sense of openness, acceptance, and community that is thought to explain why, despite stigmatization and a history of bullying, furries who identify with the furry fandom show no evidence of psychological maladaptation.

Conclusion

The members of the IARP have dedicated much time and effort to understanding the furry fandom through science. We have learned many things over the years about a group of people who are joined by their common interest in anthropomorphism. Furries have lived with the criticism of the world for many years. As the fandom grows, we hope to see general, popular acceptance grow, too. The reality is that many people participate in collective fantasy activities—some are mainstream (e.g., online gaming), others are considered deviant subcultures. While the popularity of science fiction conferences have ameliorated terms like *nerd* or *geek*, furries still experience stigma due in part to incendiary, sensationalist media portrayals which cast furries as sexual deviants. This portrayal combined with the unfamiliarity of the fandom makes many furries fear discrimination, and conventions may be one of the few places where furries may feel that they can be themselves. We hope that the work that we do will continue to inform the public about furries and make furries' choice to live authentically and without fear a reality.

References

Gerbasi, K. C., Paolone, N., Higner, J., Scaletta, L. L., Bernstein, P. L., Conway, S., & Privitera, A. (2008). Furries from A to Z (anthropomorphism to zoomorphism). Society & Animals: Journal Of HumanAnimal Studies, 16(3), 197-222. doi:10.1163/156853008X323376

Mock, S. E., Plante, C. N., Reysen, S., & Gerbasi, K. C. (2013). Deeper leisure involvement as a coping resource in a stigmatized leisure context. *Leisure/Loisir*, 37, 111-126.

Roberts, S., Plante, C., Reysen, S., & Gerbasi, K. (in press). Not all fantasies are created equal: Fantasy sport fans' perceptions of Furry, Brony, and Anime Fans. The Phoenix Papers.

Roberts, S. E., Plante, C. N., Gerbasi, K. C., & Reysen, S. (in press). Clinical interaction with anthropomorphic phenomenon: Notes for health professionals about interacting with clients who possess this unusual identity. *Health & Social Work*.

ABOUT THE ARTISTS

COVER ARTIST
Rukis Croax

Rukis is an artist and writer who has attended several furry conventions. Her art credits include the comics Cruelty, Unconditional, *and* Red Lantern. *She won an Ursa Major Award for her cover art for Kyell Gold's novel* Green Fairy. *Her own recent novel* Off the Beaten Path *also won a recent Ursa Major Award. She also created "What Lies Within," the art piece used for this book's cover.*

PROFILE ILLUSTRATION ARTIST
Sabretoothed Ermine

Ermine has been doodling cartoon animals since she was old enough to hold a pencil, and managed six years ago to make furry art her full-time job (which is lucky, as she's pretty inept at everything else). She has no formal art training (yet), but continues to learn and improve in her own slow way. She lives in beautiful BC, Canada with her husband, and enjoys reading, drinking and dnb music.

ABOUT THURSTON HOWL PUBLICATIONS

Thurston Howl Publications is a new, small publishing house in Nashville, TN. In America, it is the only furry-inclusive publisher: in other words, it is the only American publishing house that publishes both furry and non-furry works. Some of its notable works include the Amazon bestselling anthology Wolf Warriors *and Atlanta media-grabbing young adult novel* Above the Pines. *As the house continues to grow, it is always looking for new authors. If interested in learning more about Thurston Howl Publications, its publications, or its submission process, please visit us at* thurstonhowlpublications.com.

CPSIA information can be obtained
at www.ICGtesting.com
Printed in the USA
LVOW04s1603250716

497696LV00052B/1226/P